"*Faith and Fashion* is truly a masterpiece! It is unique among books today, well written, and packed with fascinating information and practical wisdom. Combining their vocational skills, Julie and Graham have researched and written a book about the Bible, fashion and clothing, and beauty, vanity, and modesty. I highly recommend this book."

—DENISE GEORGE,
bestselling author and teacher

"Fashion designer Julie Cole and systematic theologian Graham Cole believe fear-of-the-Lord wisdom extends to all of life, including the clothes we image bearers of God put on in the morning. Julie is the rare fashionista who explores the physicality of true spirituality with personal and practical advice on body type, self-image, wardrobe wisdom, and smart shopping. *Faith and Fashion* seeks to bring the inner faithful self into harmony with the fashionable self—all to the glory of God."

—DOUGLAS D. WEBSTER,
author of *Behind Nazi Lines: My Father's Heroic Quest to Save 149 World War II POWs*

"Julie's experience, creative talent, and eye for fashion and design has always left me in awe, and her love for God and his glory clearly impacts every part of her life. These two realities come together beautifully in Julie's life and ministry and are teased out in each chapter of this book, alongside Graham's theological reflections. I loved reading it and cannot imagine anyone better to write about fashion through the lens of the gospel."

—JENNY SALT,
associate to archdeacon for women's ministry, Anglican Church, Diocese of Sydney

"A true gem! This one-of-a-kind book is written by two masters of their craft: a fashion designer and a systematic theologian who also happen to be wife and husband. From Coco Chanel to Abraham Kuyper and from Francis Shaeffer to Karl Lagerfeld, this is a masterpiece of theological integration and cultural engagement. We have needed this tour de force for a long time. May it never go out of fashion!"

—C. Ben Mitchell,
Union University, emeritus

"Intrigued by the title, I read this book to discover how faith and fashion could be related. Julie and Graham have adroitly done this with humor, practical advice, and biblical information. . . . This book is an uplifting read for everyone, whether you are a fashionista and/or striving to be clothed in Christ."

—Joann Decker,
speech/language pathologist, retired

FAITH and FASHION

FAITH and FASHION

How High Is a Holy Hemline?

JULIE COLE and GRAHAM COLE

RESOURCE *Publications* • Eugene, Oregon

FAITH AND FASHION
How High Is a Holy Hemline?

Copyright © 2022 Julie Cole and Graham Cole. All rights reserved. Except for brief quotations in critical publications or reviews, no part of this book may be reproduced in any manner without prior written permission from the publisher. Write: Permissions, Wipf and Stock Publishers, 199 W. 8th Ave., Suite 3, Eugene, OR 97401.

Resource Publications
An Imprint of Wipf and Stock Publishers
199 W. 8th Ave., Suite 3
Eugene, OR 97401

www.wipfandstock.com

PAPERBACK ISBN: 978-1-6667-1652-8
HARDCOVER ISBN: 978-1-6667-1653-5
EBOOK ISBN: 978-1-6667-1654-2

AUGUST 10, 2022 10:51 AM

Scriptures taken from the Holy Bible, New International Version®, NIV®. Copyright © 1973, 1978, 1984, 2011 by Biblica, Inc.™ Used by permission of Zondervan. All rights reserved worldwide. www.zondervan.com. The "NIV" and "New International Version" are trademarks registered in the United States Patent and Trademark Office by Biblica, Inc.™

Contents

Acknowledgements | vii

Introduction | ix

Chapter 1
What's a Nice Girl Like You Doing in the Fashion Industry? | 1

Chapter 2
The Bible, Beauty, and Clothing | 13

Chapter 3
Fashion, Vanity, and Modesty | 33

Chapter 4
Wardrobe Wisdom | 49

Chapter 5
The Thoughtful Fashion Consumer | 82

Chapter 6
The Ultimate Wardrobe Change | 102

Appendix 1
What Does a Fashion Designer Do? | 107

Appendix 2
How to Build a Wardrobe the French Way | 112

Appendix 3
Sustainable Fashion | 123

Bibliography | 135

Acknowledgements

This book has been in the making for many years. It started in the USA and was finished in Australia. I have many people to thank on both continents. I am eternally grateful for their generosity and kindness in giving feedback and helpful comments on individual chapters and/or appendices and, in some cases, the entire text.

These are all gifted and wise people who have helped to make this book what it is. Some are fashionistas, theologians, teachers, or other kinds of professionals. So special thanks to Ben Mitchell, Virginia and Doug Webster, Julie Babarik, Mimika Papavasilliou, Sylvie Vanhoozer, Carol Beitzel, Amanda Maxwell, Lindsay Crenshaw, Rhonda Filmer, and especially Kati Nienas for her technical help.

These special people have helped to make this book what it is. I am ever so thankful to have you all in my life as "special" friends.

Introduction

I AM a fashion designer, and Graham is a systematic theologian. We have been blessed to have fulfilling and enjoyable careers and have flourished in them over many years. We are mutually interested in what the other does. The goal of this book is to give the reader a Christian perspective on clothing and theology by bringing our two disciplines together. I greatly benefit from our discussions on theology and what Graham is writing and teaching. We often talk about fashion as well. Writing and discussing these two topics in collaboration has been an enriching experience.

When I was speaking to a student women's group some time ago, I told them how my husband and I connect with each other's careers. I said that Graham connected with me by reading my fashion magazines, such as *Vogue*, *Elle*, and *InStyle*, even before I got to read them! Graham also proofread my fashion textbooks before their publication. I recall the time when I was struggling with a skirt I was making that was not working. I showed it to Graham. Then he suggested, "What about adding a seam in the skirt in this position?" He nailed it! Imagine my surprise that he was able to resolve my fashion problem!

The purpose of this book is to provide the Christian reader with a view of fashion that fits within a biblical framework. The questions we have asked are these: Is fashion merely a matter of vanity, superficiality, or even lust? Can I follow God and his ways and be a fashionista (i.e., someone interested in fashion)? In answering these questions, it is especially important to know how

Introduction

God sees us and what his desires for us are. As our Creator, God sees us as valuable and loved. God gives us our significance and security. Given that he loves us, he desires good things for us. However, there are times when I have been tempted to think that God did not want to give me good things. At other times, I have felt guilty pursuing fashion and wondered if it pleases God. Maybe you have also wondered similar things.

You may ask, "Well, what is fashion?" One major fashion dictionary defines fashion as "a sociocultural phenomenon in which a preference is shared by a large number of people for a particular style that lasts for a relatively short time, and then is replaced by another style."[1] Fashion can also be defined as the current style of clothing and accessories at any given time. Clothing, then, is a subset of fashion, as are accessories. For the purposes of this book, we have adopted and adapted a distinction made by Saint Augustine. This early Christian leader and thinker distinguished between things to be enjoyed, things to be used, and things to be both enjoyed and used.[2] When it comes to fashion, garments and accessories are to be enjoyed and used. For example, a jacket may be used to keep out the wind when walking but also enjoyed for its style, color, and fit. The clothing worn by a firefighter is for use. It is hard to imagine enjoying wearing gear weighing on average forty-five pounds.

Some people are not interested in fashion. This is entirely legitimate. Still, we cannot do without clothing. We have to dress whether we like it or not. We wear clothes as a covering for reasons we are all conscious of, such as modesty, protection against the elements of temperature (wind, humidity, rain), work, and leisure. Therefore, we all need to shop for clothing whether we are interested in fashion or not. What is offered in this book, whether you are a fashionista or not, are smarts about clothing wisdom in general.

This book is not only for the person who desires to have fashion smarts. It is also for anyone who wants a biblical perspective on related topics, such as beauty, modesty, body image, sustainable

---

1. Calasibetta and Tortora, *Fairchild Dictionary of Fashion*, 154.
2. Augustine, *On Christian Doctrine*, 9.

Introduction

fashion, and more. The Bible does not directly tell us how we should dress or how much makeup we should wear or how high a holy hemline is (a question we will address at a later stage in the book). However, what the Bible does give us is a framework for how we should live as people of faith. The Bible also provides a framework for thinking about beauty and God's creation. Yet another object of this book is to help Christian women be thoughtful consumers when it comes to fashion and style. As an addition to chapters 1, 2, 3, 4, and 5, Graham will offer some theological reflections. Additionally, Graham has written chapter 6, "The Ultimate Wardrobe Change." Also included are three appendices.

As women, we can easily compare ourselves with other women. Comparison thinking is prevalent today with social media like Facebook and Instagram. When I see *Vogue*'s "runway" section with slideshows of designer's latest collections, I can be tempted to feel envious of the beautiful designer clothes and wish they were mine. Even so, I do enjoy reading fashion magazines such as *Vogue*, *InStyle*, and *Harper's Bazaar* and watching celebrity shows. I love to know what people wear. Yet, these magazines are filled with photos of perfectly sculptured, beautiful women wearing fabulous clothes. We do need to be careful when exposing ourselves to unrealistic body and style images. We can find ourselves feeling pressured, dissatisfied, and enviously coveting an unrealistic body image, beautiful clothes, accessories, and jewelry. It is unrealistic to think we can have it all! However, enjoy what you see advertised in magazines and on television. But be aware that covetousness is a spoiler. It can breed discontent.

The actress Drew Barrymore struggled with her body type. She commented, "There are the 'I don't care' dressers, and then there is me: The 'I care, but I struggle with my body' type, so I wear the same things over and over."[3] Maybe you feel like this? We are all born with a certain body structure. Some of us are petite, some tall, some lean with an athletic build, some small boned and others large boned, some with a swimmer's physique. Overall, no matter what size, shape, or weight you are, it is important to find the

3. Barrymore, "Why I Put."

Introduction

"right" clothes for your body type and dress to whom you are, not to whom you are not. I know that comparing ourselves with others is one way to find out how we fit into the world. But is it a good thing to compare ourselves with tall, size-six models and what they wear on the catwalk? When we start comparing ourselves like this, we can feel dissatisfied. We need to see ourselves as God sees us.

This book is not written to make you feel dissatisfied with your height, weight, shape, or what you wear. It is quite the opposite. It is about authenticity and encouraging an acceptance of who you are.

Chapter 1: What's a Nice Girl Like You Doing in the Fashion Industry?

Just as each of us has a shape, so also does a book. In the first chapter, the content is autobiographical. It is my story of how I got into working as a fashion designer.

Chapter 2: The Bible, Beauty, and Clothing

In this chapter, the Bible, creativity, and clothing are on view. It is interesting to note that there are numerous references to clothing in the Bible, beginning with Genesis when God clothes Adam and Eve. Clothing in various categories will be discussed (priestly, ceremonial, domestic, and royal garments, among others).

Chapter 3: Fashion, Vanity, and Modesty

This chapter is shaped to draw your attention to the important topics of fashion, vanity, and modesty. Questions such as "Is looking stylish indulgent, frivolous, and worldly as a Christian?" and "How high is a holy hemline?" will be addressed.

Introduction

Chapter 4: Wardrobe Wisdom

This chapter offers key ideas for the woman who wants a general knowledge about body image, fit, color, proportion and balance, colors to suit your complexion, and ultimately, personal style. This chapter is not just theory but offers practical "how-to" style advice.

Chapter 5: The Thoughtful Fashion Consumer

This chapter is for the person who desires to be a thoughtful fashion consumer. Topics such as trends, fads, fabric savvy, and thoughtful fashion buying will be covered. Elizabeth L. Cline says, "When every garment has a purpose and every color and cut goes with something else, your wardrobe can carry you through life and style, no matter the occasion."[4]

Chapter 6: The Ultimate Wardrobe Change

The last chapter is about the most important wardrobe change of them all. The apostle Paul described it as putting on Christ like a garment (Gal 3:27). Others who came later in church history described it as being clothed in Christ's righteousness before a holy God.

Appendix 1: What Does a Fashion Designer Do?

In this appendix, the job of the fashion designer is discussed. It is a job with many facets, with creativity at its core as the designer's ideas become material reality in fabric. The designer's workplace can range from a small studio to a large factory. I have worked in both.

---

4. Cline, *Conscious Closet*, 11.

Introduction

Appendix 2: How to Build a Wardrobe the French Way

French women really know how to coordinate a well-organized, minimal wardrobe. How to dress the French way is a method of dressing worth imitating. This appendix will offer wisdom on how to do this as French women's fashion secrets are unveiled. Some other topics covered are how to declutter and downsize your wardrobe and how to build a wardrobe with key investment pieces.

Appendix 3: Sustainable Fashion

This appendix will give advice on how to build a wardrobe responsibly. Observing fashion in general, there are many concerns that relate to the clothing we buy. Topics raised in this chapter regarding sustainable fashion are environmental issues, the manufacturing of textiles, the making of clothing, and the issue of clothes that are dumped into landfills, spoiling our environment.

My hope is that this book will encourage us all, including me, to own less clothing and to face up to the fact that we own too many clothes, which ultimately are abandoned and dumped into landfills.

Our prayer is that this book will encourage you to dress to your strengths, regardless of your body imperfections (and we all have them), by wearing clothing to accent your best features. Also, throughout this book is the challenge to create a minimalist wardrobe. By doing this, you can create a more serviceable, cohesive wardrobe, which in turn creates a better life balance and less stress when getting dressed.

Our goal and vision in writing this book is to empower, encourage, and promote a wise approach to fashion. Since the God of the Bible is concerned about every detail of our lives, and this includes the clothing we wear, we want you to see that beauty and clothing can be enjoyed. You will always feel better wearing clothes you like. This can be accomplished by having fashion wisdom rather than fashion foolishness. Fashion wisdom in action

Introduction

leaves us more time to serve God and others. Such wisdom does not forgo style. We can still wear stylish, smart, eye-catching, and perhaps even cute clothing.

Chapter 1

What's a Nice Girl Like You Doing in the Fashion Industry?

> Fashion is not something that exists in dresses only. Fashion is in the sky, in the street, fashion has to do with ideas, the way we live, what is happening.
>
> COCO CHANEL

> He who works with his hands is a laborer. He who works with his hands and his head is a craftsman. He who works with his hands and his head and his heart is an artist.
>
> FRANCIS OF ASSISI

Do you feel guilty as a Christian because you love fashionable clothes? Is it wrong to enjoy material things? Is it okay to follow trends? Should I desire to look chic? Can I enjoy shopping? Can I wear nice clothes purely for enjoyment? I admit that I have an incurable love of fashion! This can create a tension, especially when the Bible tells us in Matt 6:24, "You cannot serve both God and money."

Faith and Fashion

The Dutch theologian Abraham Kuyper said, "There is not a square inch in the whole domain of our human existence over which Christ, who is Sovereign overall, does not cry, Mine!"[1] Our faith should saturate every part of our lives, and this would include our art, music, clothing, and how we dress. The challenge is to develop a healthy view of fashion so that our fashion sense and core Christian values can coexist without tension.

Clothing is important in society. As Christian followers, what, then, should our attitude be to clothing? Lucy Collins, a professor at New York's Fashion Institute of Technology, gives a reason fashion does matter. She said, "Fashion matters because our bodies matter. We're not disembodied beings existing only in a spiritual realm."[2] Fashion is ever present. We all participate in fashion each day, whether we are sleeping or working, preparing dinner, digging in the garden, or engaged in recreational activities. Clothes are valued items and a necessity in life. Clothing production is a big part of our global economy and provides jobs. Shopping keeps the global economy vibrant. Important as fashion is, shopping for clothes can bring out the worst attitude in us as consumers. It can lure us into wanting more and more material goods as new things appear.

Why do we wear clothes? We may wear clothes for several reasons. Is it to show authority, power, and class? Is it to impress or to define our identity? Is it because we like to dress up? Or do we wear clothes to disguise our body shape? Could it be because we want to draw attention to ourselves by making a fashion statement or by showing our individual aesthetic? Or is it purely for enjoyment? One main purpose for wearing clothing is to cover our bodies for the purpose of modesty. Another reason is to protect it from the elements, like wind, rain, cold, and harsh sun. Clothing is also worn to conceal. Think of camouflage for soldiers. Jopie Siebert-Hommes, a researcher in women studies, theology, and Old Testament exegesis, acknowledges the many different purposes for which clothing is worn:

1. Abraham Kuyper, qtd. in "What Is Trinity Knox," para. 3.
2. Lucy Collins, qtd. in Bauck, "Why Fashion Matters."

What's a Nice Girl Like You Doing in the Fashion Industry?

Cultural-anthropological studies emphasize that clothing is more than giving protection to the human body, it often functions as a special form of communication. It expresses a person's cultural identity, or it indicates the status, power, or gender of the wearer. In short, dress belongs to the phenomena of "body language." It is a way of making silent statements about someone's political, religious, or social standing. . . .

This applies to biblical texts as well. Heather McKay, who did some critical research concerning clothing and adornment in biblical texts, has pointed out that items of clothing frequently have an indispensable function in the development of the biblical plot. This is not only true for wearing, giving or receiving garments, but "events" such as tearing robes or covering with ash, may create pivotal points in the story as well. Without words they give a clear message to the reader. "The garments speak silently, but speak they do."[3]

Garments tell a story. What we wear can be worn to express ourselves. We can learn a lot about someone's personality and their preferences by what they wear and the colors they dress in. Leah Feldon, a fashion expert and stylist, said that before people listen to your theories, assumptions, or opinions on a variety of topics, "they will—consciously or subconsciously—judge you by your appearance."[4] When we first meet someone, what they wear makes an impression on us based on how they look in addition to their demeanor. For example, an exuberant person may wear trendy styles in bright, lively colors. Soft, pale colors, ruffles, and flounces can communicate gentleness and femininity. If we are having a bad day, we may wear dark colors.

Wearing certain types of clothing can represent different sections of society. For instance, women in India wear saris. Women in Germany and Austria wear dirndls, a full skirt gathered from the waistband. Balinese women wear a sash and "sarong-style skirt," dancers in Spain wear flamenco dresses, and women in Japan wear

---

3. Siebert-Hommes, "Symbolic Function of Clothing."
4. Feldon, *Does This Make Me*, 13.

kimonos.[5] Traditional dress for women in African countries is shaped by culture, weather, and socioeconomic standing.

Different types of clothing are also worn for religious purposes—i.e., robes, a cassock, vestments, or a clerical collar. Muslim women wear a burka to cover their bodies, which is stipulated in the Quran. A hijab head covering is also worn to conform to certain standards of modesty.

Clothing can indicate your occupation as a doctor, nurse, priest, or police officer. Clothing can show social status, such as queen, king, princess, and prince. Special clothing is worn on significant occasions. A bride wears a wedding dress, and a grieving spouse may wear black. For their First Communion, girls wear white dresses. In Jewish circles, a special dress is worn by girls celebrating their bat mitzvah. Uniforms are also made by the apparel industry for the workforce and for safety purposes. For instance, in hazardous conditions, firefighters wear special protective clothing. For protection, police wear bulletproof vests, and road workers wear fluorescent vests for identification when working in a construction zone.

Clothes can indicate a subculture within a larger culture: goth, grunge, punk, hip-hop, preppy, and biker, to name a few. In the early nineties, major bands such as Nirvana, Pearl Jam, and Sound Garden influenced a subculture style of dress. It was the grunge-era of fashion and appeared on the runway and sold in major chain stores. I know the style well. Our two sons were into the grunge style in their teenage years. The trend was all about low-budget anti-fashion—torn jeans, flannel shirts, and unkempt hair.

Now, how is it that I know all this? I am interested in fashion both personally and professionally, which brings me to my story.

---

5. Park, "Traditional Dress," paras. 3, 7, 9, 27, 40.

What's a Nice Girl Like You Doing in the Fashion Industry?

My Story

I have worked in the garment industry for over forty years. As a fashion designer and a committed follower of Christ, I find great satisfaction in creating beautiful clothing for people. During my childhood in Australia, my parents took me and my siblings to church every Sunday. (On most Sundays, my parents would have guests in our home to share a roast-lamb dinner. They practiced great Christian hospitality.) In that era—the late fifties and early sixties—women dressed up and wore high-heeled shoes to church. To avoid indentations from heel tips on wood floors, guests were required to remove their shoes and place them in our parents' bedroom. Women would also remove their Sunday hats and lay them on my parents' bed. How perfect for my sister, Carol, and I, as this meant we could play dress-up! Unobtrusively, we would go into my parents' bedroom and slip on a pair of high-heeled shoes and a hat of our choice. On other occasions, we would wear dress-up clothes, hats, beads, jewelry, and handbags—but no makeup, as it was forbidden. In our heeled shoes, we would shuffle over to the home of our neighbor, Mrs. May. She would greet us by saying, "Hello ladies, how nice of you to call. Do come in for a cup of tea." How delightful it was that she took us so seriously!

My mother loved fashion and instilled a love of fashion in my sister and me. My mother spent her evenings sewing dresses for us to wear for Christmas celebrations and other special occasions. I carefully observed what she was doing. By the time I reached the age of ten, I could sew without having to take lessons. I had a God-given natural talent for which I am so grateful. My father was a plumber and worked with his hands. He had a creative spirit! I remember sitting with him at the dining-room table as we penciled sketches together. During my college days, I recall needing a brass buckle of a particular size for a certain design. But I could not find the exact one I was looking for, so my father, using his creative skill, crafted the perfect buckle in his workshop. I observed how carefully he soldered it to my specifications to seamlessly fit my belt.

As I grew up, my creativity was encouraged and taken seriously by my parents. By the time I reached my teenage years, it was evident that God had gifted me with a set of creative abilities. I was also aware of my artistic flare associated with fashion. My parents saw value in my creativity and supported my pursuing a fashion career. I grew up in a fundamentalist church where it was a sin to swim on Sunday, drink alcohol, go to movies, dance, and wear makeup. There was a strict dress code. For example, we could not wear pants, because Deut 22:5 says, "A woman shall not wear man's clothing." Men were also forbidden to wear shorts to church or any church-related function. Yet, clothing was also important in such a "strict" church setting. Thank you, Lord! I recall feeling excited to get to church each Sunday morning. Was it to worship and learn about God? No! It was to see who was wearing a new outfit that day, including a glam hat! Why was clothing so important? We were told to dress in such a way that you could meet the queen of England. If you were prepared to dress up for the queen, then why not for the King of kings? Another reason for dressing in stylish, fashionable clothes was that it was one way for women in my church to express themselves and to be noticed, because they had to be "silent" in church.

What began as a craft for me—simply sewing—transformed into a career. By age sixteen, I had applied to design school. I entered college to study fashion design in Sydney, Australia. It mystifies me to this day why my parents did not attempt to block my fashion ambition. When I think of the church environment I grew up in, I knew going into the fashion industry could be challenging and not easy for a committed Christian. I am so thankful for my parents' encouragement in my creative pursuits to use my God-given gift to dress women in beautiful clothing. They knew it was a worthy calling and that I could honor God in my job. The verse in Col 3:17 was lived out in my parents' lives: "And whatever you do, whether in word of deed, do it all in the name of the Lord Jesus . . ." Their values were passed onto me, and so this verse became important to me as well.

What's a Nice Girl Like You Doing in the Fashion Industry?

I met my husband, Graham, in 1967 while I was in design school. He was in his last year of high school when he became a Christian. Graham went on to pursue a BA at Sydney University and was involved in a campus ministry. During this time, he attended many lectures by professors from Moore Theological College. This had a significant impact on Graham, so much so that he felt called to ministry. In 1971, we married. Yes, I did design and make my wedding dress, bridesmaid dresses, and flower girl's dress. In 1973, Graham entered Moore Theological College to train as an Anglican minister. We were both committed to this calling. Our commitment to this ministry did not mean I had to forgo my fashion career and work in the church office. I continued to pursue fashion and doing what I loved, but with a shift in outlook. I knew my career as a fashion designer would need to be flexible and fit in with church ministry. We knew we could end up living anywhere in the world. In fact, Graham has taught systematic theology in Australia, England, and the USA.

The catalyst for writing this book was a conversation that took place some forty-six years ago. I have never forgotten the dialogue! It was at a picnic connected to Moore Theological College, when I was asked a question by a prominent Anglican minister: "What do you do for a living?" "I am a fashion designer," I proudly replied. He then looked at me intently and said, "What on earth would you want to do that for?" I knew instantly that he thought that because I was not formally working in "gospel ministry" that my work had no value. Had I just been challenged to think that my creative talent had no value? Scripture tells me in Gen 1:27 that God created us male and female in God's own image. If we are created in God's image, we are formed as creators just like God.

The minister's words could have discouraged me to the point of never pursuing my profession out of guilt. I also knew there would be many challenges working as a designer in the cutthroat fashion business, but I felt prepared. I recognized that creating clothing was not a frivolous activity. Perhaps this minister thought we should all walk around naked. Instead of feeling deflated by this conversation, I felt empowered! I knew that the creative arts and entertainment, fashion, art, photography, theater, and music, just to name a few, could be significant in pointing people toward Jesus. Instantly, I determined I would become the best fashion designer I could and be an influence for good wherever I worked within the industry.

Many years later, while listening to a sermon in an Anglican church in Melbourne, Australia, it was made clear once again that working in formal gospel ministry was regarded as the only occupation that really matters in God's sight. Working outside of formal gospel ministry was less valuable. However, Jas 1:17 tells us that every gift is from God. They are not our own. Tim Keller has said, "If you have money, power, and status today, it is due to the century and place in which you were born, to your talents, capacities, and health, none of which you earned. In short, all your resources are in the end the gift of God."[6]

I knew I was being true to the unique person God had created me to be by pursuing a vocation in fashion. Certainly, there are times when our job may be difficult. We may experience stressful relationships and job dissatisfaction because of the demands made on us. For these reasons, we may need to change our job or career direction because it is not a good fit. Despite this, according to Col 3:23–24, we are to take the Bible's claim about work seriously. We are to work hard and do excellent work with all intelligence and vigor, because it is Christ we are serving. I find it important to follow the wisdom taught in Prov 16:3: "Commit your work to the Lord, and your plans will be established." One day, my boss called me to ask if I had arrived at work. I was sitting in my car in the parking lot. "I've arrived early," I said. "I'm sitting in my car praying about my day's work." She was amazed to think that I would pray and ask God to help me do excellent work that day.

---

6. Keller, "If you have money."

How Is My Faith Expressed in My Work as a Fashion Designer?

I have learned over the years that my work as fashion designer can coexist with a faith-filled life. As Leighton Ford said, "Our personal lives and our vocational lives are woven together as part of God's great pattern."[7] How I perform within the fashion industry is important, and how I conduct myself matters. In the same way, whether you work in sales, you are a trusted dog walker, or you are a teacher or academic, your work is to reflect the character of Christ. Being a child of God should shape how we behave. The privilege of being God's children also brings a responsibility to walk in God's ways. Every sphere of our work is to mirror God's character. Ephesians 2:10 tells us that we are "God's handiwork, created in Christ Jesus to do good works, which God prepared for us to do in advance."

Fashion designer Enoch Ho knows this. He was intentional in the way he used his gifts in service to God: "I believe we don't have to separate business and charity, work and good deeds. It can be both."[8] Ho believes that his work as a fashion designer and his contribution to society are not unrelated but rather go hand in hand. In the same way, our son Jerome, who lives in Melbourne, is a wedding photographer and sees shooting a wedding as service to God by the way he serves his clients with his artistry and by his manner. Tim Keller said, "If God's purpose for your job is that you serve the human community, then the way to serve God best is to do the job as well as it can be done."[9]

My responsibility is to do my work well and be an influence for good as well as to empower others to flourish in the workplace. I am to live according to the fruit of the Spirit in Gal 5:22–23, that of "love, joy, peace, forbearance, kindness, goodness, faithfulness, gentleness and self-control" expressed in thoughts, emotions, and feelings. These values are to characterize my life. In my work, I

---

7. Ford, *Life of Listening*, 178.
8. Enoch Ho, qtd. in Cheng-Tozun, "Enoch Ho," para. 4.
9. Tim Keller, qtd. in Yeoman, "24/7 Faith," para. 33.

value the personhood and humanity of every person I interact with regardless of their background, religion, gender, or sexuality. I recall teaching a cross-dresser how to sew. Whether it was Chanel or Brian who arrived that day to class, I kindly took his/her hands to position them in the right place to sew. At other times, I would sit alongside my college students and listen as they told me their stories of adversity and dysfunction. My responsibility in my work, regardless of what I do, is to exemplify Christ. I am to care for, love, value, and respect each person within my orbit.

Where Am I Today?

I am very thankful for a career in fashion and for the encouragement I received from my Christian parents. I have designed many collections; traveled the world; worked in haute couture, ready-to-wear, and custom-made clothing; taught in fashion-design programs in three different colleges; written textbooks and articles; and tutored students in fashion-related subjects. At present, I still work in the fashion industry. Yet, the pinnacle of my work was to create my daughter's beautiful blush-pink Schiffli lace wedding dress. I beaded the lace hour by hour, day by day, and month by month with Swarovski crystals, rose gold, and freshwater pearls. Every stitch and embellishment were creating beauty as this gorgeous gown evolved. Did it bring me joy? Oh yes, extraordinary joy and satisfaction! It also brought joy to many others as they watched Hannah walk down the aisle arm in arm with her husband-to-be, Victor, in this gorgeous gown.

Even though my husband, Graham, and I were dedicated to Christian ministry, God has provided creative work for me to be involved in as well. I am still 100 percent committed to my craft. I thank the Lord for my calling to create clothing and the opportunity to integrate my vocation with my faith. I know that my creative talent as a fashion designer *is* a gift from God and that God values it. Every avenue of the arts belongs to God, even fashion. Surely, as a fashion designer I have permission to experience joy as I create beautiful clothes and to do it to the glory of God.

Some of my biblical discoveries in the following chapter validate my work as a fashion designer. But before looking at these discoveries, I am interested in knowing what Graham thinks about the value of my work as fashion designer.

Worship and Work: A Reflection by Graham

Jules, I am struck by the picture of God in the opening chapters of the Bible (Gen 1–2). He comes before us as the great Worker: six days on the job and then a day off. He creates us in his image in chapter 1, and we see what that looks like as Adam cares for the garden in chapter 2. We should not be surprised, then, to find that we need to work. Think about it—the incarnate Son of God worked with wood as an artisan as well as with the spoken word as a preacher. And by work, I do not mean just paid work. I mean doing worthwhile stuff, whether paid or not. We are also created to worship. Jesus taught us that the Father is seeking worshipers. Is there a connection, though, between work and worship, or are these activities in compartments sealed off from each other? I recall a sign outside a church which stated that divine worship was to take place at 10:00 a.m. on Sunday mornings. Now, in a sense, that is obviously right. God's people gather and express the worth of God in words spoken and sung. This is corporate worship. We see it in a psalm like Ps 149:1: "Praise the Lord. Sing to the Lord a new song, his praise in the assembly of his faithful people." We also see it in Rev 4–5, where a heavenly scene is depicted in which all sorts of creatures express together the worth of God.

However, there is another aspect to worship that Saint Paul writes about. It is our life lived in response to the gospel: "Therefore, I urge you, brothers and sisters, in view of God's mercy, to offer your bodies as a living sacrifice, holy and pleasing to God—this is your true and proper worship" (Rom 12:1). This is mindblowing. What you do as a mother or a father or an accountant or a pastor or a fashion designer, offered to God for his glory, is New Testament worship in this broad sense. Sunday connects to Monday through this idea of worship. But what exactly does it look like? How does an idea become more than just a notion rattling around in our heads? It seems to me that prayer is the key. Do we begin each day offering our work and what we do in it to the Lord? That is what Jules and I do at breakfast. We offer our work to God: my work as dean of a divinity school and your work as a writer and fashion designer. Saint Paul put it this way in Col 3:23–24: "Whatever you do, work at it with all your heart, as working for the Lord, not for human masters, since you know that you will receive an inheritance from the Lord as a reward. It is the Lord Christ you are serving." The great reformer of the sixteenth century Martin Luther captured that biblical truth when he preached the following:

> The prince should think: Christ has served me and made everything to follow him; therefore, I should also serve my neighbor, protect him and everything that belongs to him. That is why God has given me this office, and I have it that I might serve him. That would be a good prince and ruler. When a prince sees his neighbor oppressed, he should think: That concerns me! I must protect and shield my neighbor. . . . The same is true for shoemaker, tailor, scribe, or reader. If he is a Christian tailor, he will say: I make these clothes because God has bidden me do so, so that I can earn a living, so that I can help and serve my neighbor. When a Christian does not serve the other, God is not present; that is not Christian living.[10]

Jules found that she can design and make clothes in the service of others to the glory of God. Her Sundays and Mondays connect.

---

10. Martin Luther, "Sermon in the Castle Church at Weimar," qtd. in Gaiser, "What Luther Didn't Say," 361.

Chapter 2

The Bible, Beauty, and Clothing

> If that is how God clothes the grass of the field, which is here today and tomorrow thrown into the fire, will he not much more clothe you—you of little faith?
>
> MATT 6:30

> I believe the world is incomprehensively beautiful—an endless prospect of magic and wonder.
>
> ANSEL ADAMS

MANY artists question their creative work and wonder if it has value. Guggi is just one artist who doubted if art was worthwhile and meaningful. He is one of Ireland's most celebrated contemporary artists. Interestingly, Guggi grew up on the same street as Bono in Dublin. Bono (his stage name) is the lead singer and primary lyricist of the rock band U2. Together they shared a love of art and music and experienced a similar spiritual upbringing. Both are "believers" and came to faith through their fathers.[1]

Guggi comments:

---

1. Falsani, "Bono and Guggi."

I've drawn and painted since I was a child, and I kind of started feeling guilty about it—what am I adding here? What am I bringing to society? . . . But then this preacher at my grandmother's funeral said, "If we are created in God's image, we must in some way be like him. And if God is the creator, we must also be creative." That just struck a chord with me—that art isn't just enough to do, it's a special thing to do. I feel incredibly privileged to be able to paint, to be able to make pictures and sculptures. . . . I'm merely a channel, and it comes through me and I'm available for service in that sense.[2]

The Impact of Edith Schaeffer

In the seventies as a young fashion designer, I also questioned if my talent and creativity was worthwhile and if clothing in general had value. At the same time, Graham was in seminary and I was surrounded by academia. In this context, I wondered if my creativity was respected and had equal worth in God's sight as that of an intellectual's gifts and talent. So I began reading Edith Schaeffer's book *Hidden Art*. I soon realized that Schaffer was ahead of her time. This book changed my life. It offered me wisdom and practical application as an artist. She drew her ideas from the Bible. She emphasized the fact that we were created in the image of God, who is the artistic Creator.[3] So, whether we are Christians or not, God gives us inborn gifts (talents). Schaeffer's writing gave me permission to create the beautiful, to live artistically and aesthetically, whether creating a space at home or creating fashion. Indeed, a painting, photograph, or beautifully crafted dress can point us to the source of all beauty. His formation of the heavens and earth was his creation to give us pleasure (Col 1:16–17). God the Creator gave us sight to see color, tint and shade, dimension, size, shape,

---

2. Falsani, "Bono and Guggi," paras. 31, 37.
3. Schaeffer, *Hidden Art*.

The Bible, Beauty, and Clothing

and proportion, as well as the ability to feel and appreciate texture from the earth's formation.

Several high-profile people from varied walks of life testify to the significance of creativity being an important part of our humanity. Educationalist Sir Ken Robinson argued, "Creativity is as important now in education as literacy, and we should treat it with the same status."[4] This fact should not surprise us, as we are made in God's image. Rosalind Picard, professor of media arts and science at the Massachusetts Institute of Technology, in her search for truth decided she needed to read the Bible. In her testimony, she said, "I once thought I was too smart to believe in God. Now I know I was an arrogant fool who snubbed the greatest Mind in the cosmos—the Author of all science, mathematics, art, and everything else there is to know."[5] Nicola Brown, an international writer, editor, and communications specialist, also writes convincingly about the impact of creativity in a society and, indeed, the whole world:

> The continual challenge is that creativity and the arts have a tendency to be looked at as a decorative addition on top of the critical social, economic, and political fabric of a thriving society rather than an essential part of the picture. This is fundamentally misguided. Creativity is closely linked to our ability to problem solve, express ourselves freely, reflect critically, and achieve personal fulfillment and self-actualization. You could easily argue that these are the building blocks of a society's social, economic, and political success.[6]

Over time, I realized that my artistic talent had value, just as academia had value. Edith Schaeffer was a great encouragement to me to pursue my artistic talent, because every good and perfect gift is from a generous God. I knew clothing is a necessity in society and that someone must create clothes. So why not me? First Timothy 6:7 tells us of the necessity of clothing: "For we

---

4. Ken Robinson, qtd. in Oleic, "Why Creativity," para. 2.
5. Picard, "An MIT Professor," para. 17.
6. Brown, "Why Creative Thinkers," para. 4.

brought nothing into the world, and we can take nothing out of it. But if we have food and clothing, we will be content with that." To express my creativity, while Graham was studying theology, I decorated our small nineteenth-century, four-roomed house (with a backyard outhouse) in popular 1970s colors (orange, lime green, brown, and red). We took pleasure in our surroundings. Our little house was colorful and rocked with the beat of the Beatles! Administration often brought prospective students by to look at our little Newtown home (in Sydney, Australia) and the creative way it was decorated. Our creative pursuits can bless and delight.

Celebrating Life

It is clear in Scripture that we can enjoy and celebrate life. As Christians, we can enjoy food and wine, movies, shopping, and clothes. It is about balance; if we love these things more than God, then our priorities are not balanced. Recently, in the Anglican church we attend, we all read Ps 104. Verse 26 struck me: "There the ships go to and fro, and Leviathan [probably the whale], which you formed to frolic there." So, God created this animal to enjoy the sea! Similarly, God has made us to enjoy each other and the world he has created. In Neh 8:10, Nehemiah told the people to remember God's grace in their lives by celebrating. He said, "Go and enjoy choice food and sweet drinks, and send some to those who have nothing prepared. This day is sacred to our Lord. Do not grieve, for the joy of the LORD is your strength" (Neh 8:10). John's Gospel also tells us the story of the wedding at Cana in Galilee (John 2:1–12). Jesus, his mother, and the disciples were invited to the wedding celebration. Jesus' mother was concerned because the wine had run out. This would dampen any celebration! As the story unfolds, we see Jesus perform a miracle by turning six stone water jars into wine so the guests could continue to enjoy the wedding feast. It was customary to serve the best wine first so the guests could delight in the provision given by the host. Jesus turned tradition around

The Bible, Beauty, and Clothing

and supplied the best wine last.[7] This miracle was performed to manifest God's glory.

Some clothing we read about in Scripture is planned by God with exactness regarding the designs, distinct materials to be used, specific colors, and embellishments worn for a particular purpose and for aesthetic beauty. This shows us that the God of the Bible is concerned about every detail of our lives, including clothing worn in biblical days. Part of the celebration of life can also be to enjoy and get pleasure from clothing, color, and beauty. I believe that dressing nicely can give pleasure to the wearer and be pleasurable to the viewer. A few of my friends have commented on how they feel a sense of joy when seeing how I style myself.

In the book of Ruth, we read the delightful short story of how Ruth's mother-in-law, Naomi, instructs her to complete some beauty treatments so she looks attractive dressed as a bride. She instructs Ruth to wash, put on perfume, and dress in her best outfit on the evening of her betrothal to Boaz (Ruth 3:3). Indeed, what a delight for Boaz! In this beautiful story, Boaz is the family's kinsman-redeemer. Some scholars think that this fact points to Jesus being our ultimate Redeemer.[8]

My friend Rhonda was telling me the story of how someone in her church admired the beauty of the bracelet she was wearing. Some years earlier, I had given it to her as a birthday gift because I knew it would suit her dressing style. It may have been the color, design, texture, or shape that appealed to the person and gave pleasure and enjoyment. Doesn't God want us to enjoy beauty, even when it is just a bracelet? What has value in our lives? Doesn't going to the ballet or listening to Mozart's Symphony No. 41 have value? The fact is that we can delight in and enjoy God's world of innovation, creativity, clothing and costumes, stage and sets, tunes, and movements.

---

7. Kruse, *John*, 99.
8. For example, see Chase, "True and Greater Boaz."

FAITH AND FASHION

Clothing in the Bible

Recently, on a visit to an airport, I saw so many different types of clothing. Some wore military uniforms; some wore business attire; some wore very, very casual everyday outfits; some had clerical collars; and some wore . . . I just do not know what to call it. How fascinating, then, to read my Bible and find so many of the same kinds of clothing: military, everyday, and religious. Wedding dresses and royal robes are in the Bible too. I did not see any wedding dresses or royal robes as I waited for my flight, but there they were in the magazines on the newsstands.

Before looking more closely at what the Bible has to say about clothing, creativity, and God's relationship to beauty, we need to make an important distinction between fashion and clothing. All fashion is clothing, but not all clothing is fashion. For example, a police uniform is clothing worn to identify a person entrusted with authority; it is not fashion. The Bible does not directly address fashion; even so, the Bible does have a lot to say about clothing. Clothing in the Bible is both utilitarian and role specific. For example, Genesis speaks of Adam and Eve wearing garments of skin and John the Baptist, the "dapper" dresser, wearing camel's hair and a leather belt. We also read of other utilitarian garments such as cloaks, robes, tunics, and undergarments. Then there are royal garments—some exceptionally fine, ornate garments with embellishments, such as gold interwoven into fabric, which signify status.

There are numerous references to various garments in the Bible. I would love to discuss all of them. If I did that, after some time, you would be saying, "Overkill!" So only a few biblical references will be featured and discussed in this section. As already mentioned, in the first book of the Bible, we find that after the fall, God clothed Adam and Eve in garments made from skin (Gen 3:21). These are the first garments we read of in the Bible. After Adam and Eve had eaten the forbidden fruit, they were aware that they were naked. As a remedy, they stitched fig leaves together to cover their nakedness. Then they hid from God. Genesis goes

The Bible, Beauty, and Clothing

on to tell us how God created clothing for them: "The LORD God made garments of skin for Adam and his wife and clothed them" (Gen 3:21). You could say that God was the first clothing provider. Interestingly, one of my great interests as a designer is working with leather skins.

Joseph is an outstanding Bible character. As a young man, Joseph's ornate coat (robe), which was a gift from Jacob, his father, took on a special meaning (Gen 37:3). It signified his special standing within the family. We often imagine Joseph's coat to be an array of multicolored patchwork material. However, we do not know the exact style. Later in life, Joseph so impressed pharaoh that he was put in charge of the whole land of Egypt. His role was noteworthy and significant. His clothing reflected his important role. Genesis 41:42 tells us: "Then Pharaoh dressed him in robes of fine linen and put a gold chain around his neck."

Skilled workers with God-given talent and ability made priestly garments for Moses' brother, Aaron—the high priest—and his sons to wear as they carried out their priestly duties (Exod 28). Leviticus 8:7 lists them: a tunic tied with a sash, a robe, and an ephod fastened with a decorative waistband tied around his waist. The sacred garments for Aaron signified dignity and honor upon his consecration, which set him apart to serve as a priest. The Lord gave Moses the precise style specifications, color palette, fabric requirements, and embellishment details. The following instructions sound like a design brief I might have received as part of my job as a fashion designer:

> Make the ephod of gold, and of blue, purple, and scarlet yarn, and of finely twisted linen—the work of skilled hands. It is to have two shoulder pieces attached to two of its corners, so it can be fastened. Its skillfully woven waistband is to be like it—of one piece with the ephod and made with gold, and with blue, purple, and scarlet yarn and with finely twisted linen. . . . They made the robe of the ephod entirely of blue cloth—the work of a weaver—with an opening in the center of the robe like the opening of a collar, and a band around this opening, so that it would not tear. They made pomegranates

of blue, purple, and scarlet yarn and finely twisted linen around the hem of the robe. And they made gold bells of pure gold and attached them around the hem between the pomegranates. The bells and the pomegranates alternated around the hem of the robe to be worn for ministering as the Lord commanded Moses. (Exod 28:6–8, 39:22–26)

I imagine that Aaron's coordinated priestly garments would have been splendid to look at as he served in God's tabernacle. Aaron's garments were not purely utilitarian but were also for glory and beauty, which can be seen in the decorative features such as pomegranates and bells. Clearly, God was Aaron's clothing designer. Indeed, God delights in the beautiful!

Not all garments mentioned in Scripture had spiritual significance. Some clothing was worn for pure pleasure or for enjoyment or simply as a covering. I delight in reading the story of Samuel as a boy serving in the temple. First Samuel 2:19 tells of how Hannah, Samuel's mother, made a little robe for her son. Every year, Hannah took the garments to Samuel on her way to the hill country of Ephraim to offer her annual sacrifice. I cannot see any theological significance in gifting the robe to Samuel each year. Yet, Scripture mentions it. I imagine the robes had great family significance as beautiful human handiwork passed from a mother to her son.

Scripture also mentions clothing worn by royalty. Queen Esther wore royal robes in the same way Her Majesty Queen Elizabeth dresses on official occasions in her royal robe, jewels, and crown. In Esth 5:1, we read, "On the third day Queen Esther put on her royal robes and stood in the inner court of the palace in front of the king's court." We do not have the exact description of her fine clothes, but obviously, Esther dressed regally, as a queen would. It is interesting to note that Queen Elizabeth's stately robe is a cape with an extensive, eighteen-foot velvet train weighing fifteen pounds. I wonder if Queen Esther's royal robe was as magnificent as Queen Elizabeth II's.

Some garments had significant spiritual meaning. After the death of Jesus, the soldiers divided his clothes into four shares to

The Bible, Beauty, and Clothing

give a portion to each of the four soldiers in the execution squad. The soldiers kept his seamless undergarment (tunic). John 19:23 describes it as "woven in one piece from top to bottom." They did not slash it into four pieces, because it had value. Instead, they cast lots for it. They were not the slightest bit aware that they were fulfilling the Davidic prophecy found in Ps 22:18: "They divide my clothes among them and cast lots for my garments." Additionally, high priests wore this type of undergarment. The first-century Jewish historian Josephus states, "Now this vesture was not composed of two pieces, nor was it sewed together upon the shoulders and the sides, but it was one long vestment so woven as to have an aperture for the neck."[9] It is significant that Jesus wore a seamless undergarment to the cross beneath his outer clothing. An intriguing suggestion is that it symbolizes an association with the seamless undergarments worn by high priests in the temple. After Christ's death on the cross and his resurrection, he now serves as our "great high priest," as Heb 4:14 tells us.[10]

Garments can also be made to serve others. Dorcas in Acts 9:36–43 was a person who did acts of service by doing good to others and helping the poor. Scripture tells us that she became sick and died. Peter was urged to "please come at once" (Acts 9:38). When he arrived, all the widows stood around crying and showing him the robes and other clothing that Dorcas had made while she was with them. Her craft was obviously valued by the early Christian community.

Materials, Embellishments, and Embroidery

Materials and textures of clothing such as sackcloth, linen and wool, camel's hair, embroidery, and much more are intertwined throughout Scripture. Material was used as a physical covering, but it could also have symbolic, moral, or spiritual importance. There are many references in the Bible that speak about wearing

---

9. Lane, "High Priest," para. 5.
10. Lane, "High Priest," para. 6.

sackcloth. Sackcloth was thick and coarsely woven material made from goats' hair, which would have felt rough and course on the skin and extremely uncomfortable to wear. This outward garb was worn as a symbol of sorrow, distress, or mourning or a sign of repentance. For example, Daniel wore sackcloth and ashes to signify deep grief and mourning. He bowed before the Lord, pleading for Israel's forgiveness and restoration because they had transgressed and been unfaithful (Dan 9:3). We also read about Hezekiah, who tore his clothes and put on sackcloth before he went into the temple to ask the Lord to save Jerusalem (2 Kgs 19:1).

You may recognize that the same natural fibers are used for clothing today that were used for clothing so long ago. Natural fibers derived from plants and animals are used for clothing in the Bible. Linen made from flax plants is one of the oldest fabrics used by humans. For example, in ancient Egypt, the making of fine linen was well known. In ancient Egypt, flax was grown on the banks of the River Nile and was known for its export trade.[11] The Bible often mentions linen for clothing. A particularly significant passage is in Revelation. It tells us how worshipers will ultimately be dressed as a bride wearing radiant garments: "For the wedding of the Lamb has come, and his bride has made herself ready. Fine linen, bright and clean, was given her to wear" (Rev 19:7–8).[12] Fine linen stands for the righteous acts of God's holy people.[13]

The spinning and weaving of linen were skills the Hebrews and Canaanite women learned from Egyptian women. The art of spinning and weaving was a highly prized job. In Exod 35:25, skilled women spun blue, purple, or scarlet yarn and fine linen materials for use in the tabernacle. In Esth 8:15, Mordecai wore royal blue and white garments and a purple robe of fine linen when in the presence of King Xerxes. The woman in Prov 31 depicts a wife with dignified character. Her life embodies godliness and wisdom.

---

11. In chapter 5, the topic of fabric is discussed at more length.

12. This is the ultimate wardrobe change that will be talked about by Graham in chapter 6.

13. See Brian J. Tabb's footnote on Rev 19:8 in Carson, *NIV Study Bible*, 2308.

The Bible, Beauty, and Clothing

She has outstanding creative skills and works with eager hands. She herself dresses in clothing made from fine linen and purple. She also selects wool and flax and creates and sells linen garments. Perhaps she is a fashion designer, and certainly a businessperson!

Linen was not only used for clothing but also for other purposes. We read in John 19:40 that after the death of Jesus, Joseph the disciple, accompanied by Nicodemus, took Jesus' body. Jesus' body was then wrapped in strips of linen cloth that were mixed with myrrh and aloes.

The only mention of silk (spun from the silkworm) is in the account of the fall of Babylon, the commercial center of the world. Revelation 18:12 speaks about the lament over Babylon and how no one will buy their cargo of "fine linen, purple, silk and scarlet cloth." Verse 16 says, "Woe! Woe to you, great city, dressed in fine linen, purple and scarlet, and glittering with gold, precious stones and pearls!" Other luxuries and all the wealth in Babylon would vanish, and merchants of the earth would weep and mourn for her.

Wool fibers are also mentioned in Scripture. Abel raised sheep in Gen 4:2, and David—as the youngest son of Jesse—was the family shepherd in 1 Sam 16:11. Wool fleece (from sheep) had many uses. One use was that it was woven into garments. Desirable fleece was to be as white as snow. To achieve this, it first needed to be washed in a brook and then cleansed with soap. We read in Isa 1:18: "'Come now, let us settle the matter,' says the LORD. 'Though your sins are like scarlet, they shall be as white as snow; though they are red as crimson, they shall be like wool.'" What beautiful similes these are in Isaiah! Ultimately, our fundamental cleansing is dependent on another—namely, Christ's sacrifice for us.

Embroidery is an embellishment. It was needlework done by skilled hands. For example, we read in Exod 39:30 the precise design details for the sash Aaron the priest was to wear: "The sash was made of finely twisted linen and blue, purple and scarlet yarn [the work of an embroiderer] as the Lord commanded Moses." The embroidery, with its vibrant colors of intertwined linen threads, was a magnificent decorative embellishment on the sash. It is interesting to note that the three main colors of fine, intertwined, twisted linen were the same colors (blue, purple, and scarlet) used for the creation of ten curtains in the tabernacle with cherubim (heavenly beings) woven into them (Exod 26:1). Moses inspected the decorative objects, accessories, and sacred garments to be used for worship. Moses blessed all who had worked in accordance with the Lord's instructions (Exod 39:32–34). Paul S. Williamson enlightens us here when he writes that Moses' blessing was "echoing God's blessing of the seventh day after his work of creation" in Gen 2:3.[14] God is undoubtedly into beautiful details!

The Israelites were instructed to embellish their garments with tassels. A tassel is made from loosely hanging threads or cords and is knotted at one end. The description of these tassels is found in Num 15:37–41. The Lord instructed Moses to tell the Israelites that they were to create tassels from blue cord and attach them to the corners of the garments. The tassels were to be a reminder to obey the commands of the Lord and to be totally dedicated to the Lord. Perhaps today when people wear a cross necklace or a T-shirt with a cross, it can also be a reminder to obey the Lord's commands.

Interestingly, Jesus knew how fabric behaves. In this case, it is sewing wisdom. Jesus said in Mark 2:21, "No one sews a patch of unshrunk cloth on an old garment. Otherwise, the new piece will pull away from the old, making the tear worse." I certainly know this to be true as a seamstress.

Makeup and Hair

God expects us to take good care of our bodies because they are part of his creation. We must nurture and celebrate our body, yet not make an idol of our appearance. Even good things, such as sport and fitness, can become an idol. Taking care of our bodies involves maintaining the largest organ, our skin. Looking after your skin has many health benefits and is just as important as food and drink. I have read repeatedly the importance of using a good

---

14. Paul R. Williamson, footnote on Exod 39:32–43 in Carson, *NIV Study Bible*, 170.

The Bible, Beauty, and Clothing

daily skin-care routine to sustain a glowing complexion. For some, it may be exfoliating and using sunblock, a good moisturizer, eye cream, and oil to nourish your skin. Maintaining your skin should not be considered vanity. It is part of valuing and caring for yourself.

We also read of skin care in the Bible. Even King David knew the importance of looking after his skin. We read in 2 Sam 12:20: "Then David got up from the ground. After he had washed, put on lotions and changed his clothes, he went into the house of the Lord and worshiped." The book of Esther tells us about her beauty treatment. Before any young woman was paraded before King Xerxes, (the Persian king) they required twelve months of beautifying treatment (Esth 2:12). The first six months involved oil and myrrh therapy, followed by another six months of unique perfume and ointment treatments. (I checked online and found that frankincense, myrrh perfumes, and incense fragrances are still on the market today.) King Xerxes was more attracted to Esther than the other young women, and she was taken to the king's palace. Because he loved her, he set a royal crown on her head and made her queen (Esth 2:17). Was it her beauty treatment alone that turned the king's head toward Esther? No, it was also Esther's grace and kindness that triumphed and found favor with the king. As the story unfolds, we read about her disposition. Queen Esther was able to intercede on behalf of the Jewish people by petitioning for God's help to save her people. Ultimately, it was not only her physical beauty that attracted the king but also her inner beauty of noble character which radiated from within. Physical beauty alone is not enough. If a person looks beautiful yet is spiteful and malicious in character, their beauty soon fades.

We need balance here. There should never be pressure on people to wear makeup. It is a personal choice. I was chatting with my gorgeous young friend recently about makeup in general. She felt overwhelmed with the demands of her morning routine. She wanted to look stylish but felt anxious by the pressure to apply makeup. Her desire was to look as natural as possible. I told her, "Keep your makeup routine simple." I encouraged her to find

Faith and Fashion

natural-looking products to match her skin tone and to enhance her features. I suggested an effortless way forward. Think about choosing three essentials to use for a natural look. Perhaps it's blush, mascara, and lip gloss; or mascara, lipstick, and a bronzer; or mascara, blush, and concealer. Three basic products can provide a natural look. It is more economical and will save time, especially for a busy person. If you are a mother who is trying to get out of the door each morning, then your makeup routine will look different than that of someone who does not have the responsibility of caring for children. They will have more discretionary time. When the designer Carolina Herrera was asked what she would never leave the house without, she said, "Lipstick. When I have it on, I feel perfect."[15] I agree! If wearing lipstick makes you feel good and look good, then wear it! Why not look as attractive as possible? I think unbelievers are drawn to Christians who look attractive.

If you wear makeup, choose quality products. To find the best makeup to suit your skin tone, go to a makeup counter and get a complimentary makeover. A makeup artist will choose the product colors to best suit your skin tone. Ask for samples and test them yourself.

Recently, I met a friend who was shopping for makeup at Target. She asked me what I was buying.

"Lipstick," I said. I showed her the color from the magazine clipping.

She admired the color and said, "I only buy one basic lipstick color which goes with everything."

Wow, I was impressed! As I thought about what my friend had said, I knew that I owned too many lipsticks. So I decided to narrow my supply of lipsticks to two, one in coral and the other in a pink tone. I have found this freeing! Both colors complement my complexion and the seasonal color palette of clothing I own.

There are some biblical references to makeup. As teenagers, we were told when applying makeup to be careful not to look like Queen Jezebel, the wife of King Ahab. She wore eye makeup and

---

15. Martin, "Carolina Herrera," para. 6.

The Bible, Beauty, and Clothing

arranged her hair.[16] She was known as the epitome of a wicked woman. (I am not sure what Jezebel had to do with my makeup!) Jeremiah 4:30 also refers to makeup. The passage says, "What are you doing, you devastated one? Why dress in scarlet and put on jewels of gold? Why highlight your eyes with makeup? You adorn yourself in vain. Your lovers despise you: they want to kill you." This verse is not banning makeup; neither is it prescribing whether we should or should not wear makeup. In context, though, this verse is not actually concerned about makeup. Rather, it is about Jerusalem needing to repent of her wicked ways and not put her trust in foreign lands. It depicts Jerusalem putting on glam clothes to woo her former lovers, which are Assyria and Egypt.[17]

For some, wearing makeup helps them to feel more confident and attractive. Wearing makeup may build self-confidence and merely be for enjoyment, or it may be your artistic expression. Others need to wear makeup for their profession, such as entertainers, actors, and dancers. Above all, wear makeup in a way that is authentic. Actress Beck Newton has this wise advice: "No matter how much or how little make-up I am wearing, I look in the mirror and see myself looking back. While I love the idea that fashion can transform you, you still have to look like you."[18] Overdone makeup can distract.

It is key to match your makeup with your skin color to create a facial glow. There is the fear of looking artificial—no one wants to look like they are trying too hard and especially that they are trying to look younger than they are. Your makeup should enhance *you*, not draw attention to itself.

It is also important to take good care of your hair. Luke 12:7 says, "Indeed, the very hairs of our head are all numbered." This is how much we are valued because God cares for us. Just as our bodies are individually shaped, so are our faces and our hair. When

---

16. 2 Kings 9:30 simply describes Jezebel's makeup—it does not prohibit it.
17. See Iain M. Duguid's footnote on Jer 4:30 in Carson, *NIV Study Bible*, 1299.
18. Zee and Bullock, *ELLEments of Personal Style*, 178.

you get your hair styled, the focus should be on the shape of your face and the cut suiting it.

Ultimately, your attitude is more important than your makeup. We know makeup is temporary, and it is not our true beauty. However, if your makeup is pleasing to the eye and makes you feel confident and self-assured, then go ahead and wear it!

Importantly, as a Christian, you do not want your makeup routine to dominate your life. First Peter 3:3 tells us that our beauty is not to come from our outward appearance by wearing extravagant, stylish clothes, ornate hairdos, earrings, necklaces, and bracelets. Peter does not forbid us from wearing elaborate products but instead tells us that our true source of beauty should not come from our external clothing but from within, from the unfading beauty of a calm and quiet spirit. This is beauty in God's sight.

Beauty Realism

Many of us are concerned with looking pretty and glamorous by the world's standards. We constantly see pictures in glossy magazines and on social media of perfectly made-up women who can make us feel self-critical, incomplete, and inadequate. Many of these glam photos posted are retouched images, which wrongly portray women, according to Dr. Rachel O'Neill, licensed therapist. Buying into these false images and comparing *our* appearance to theirs can lead to mental health issues. She says, "Over time, it's possible for an individual to internalize these feelings, which may result in low self-esteem, reduced self-confidence, and feelings of sadness and depression."[19] An article I read recently which is pertinent to the COVID-19 pandemic talks about how technology is impacting people because we need to perfect our self-image. (I know myself how I will make sure I look good on a Zoom call!) Dr. Hilary Weingarden, body dysmorphia expert, warns us that "over-focusing on your appearance for prolonged periods of time

---

19. Rachel O'Neill, qtd. in Flyyn, "Retouched Photos," para. 8.

can actually distort your perceptions so that you're no longer really seeing yourself clearly."[20]

It was so good to read about a law in France that came into practice in 2017. The French Ministry of Health announced, "It will be mandatory to use the label 'retouched photo' alongside any photo used for commercial purposes when the body of a model has been modified by image-editing software to either slim or flesh out her figure."[21] As women, we can be consumed by unrealistic beauty ideals. We strive to get the ideal figure, the right haircut, the ideal lip gloss, and the perfect flawless tan. There is nothing wrong with wanting to look our best. However, our aim should be to maintain vitality, health, and energy. Grace Codington, a former model and creative director of *Vogue* magazine, influenced fashion and style for decades. Hear her wise words: "Beauty is not about perfection. I prefer imperfections—it's much more interesting. . . . Perfect is boring."[22]

Conclusion

I believe we can have a sense of fun and adventure when it comes to our clothing, jewelry, makeup, and hairstyles. Yet, they should not be an idol. It is a mistake to feel guilty about taking time for yourself. Careful decisions about our clothing choices and beauty regime can be an important part of self-care and an integral part of personal well-being. We are multifaceted. We are made up of mind, body, and spirit. We must take care of ourselves so that, in turn, we can care for others. If fashion and your beautification is the full focus of your life, then this is a concern, because how we look is only an aspect of who we truly are. We can be interested and enjoy fashion and ornamentation, but we need to be interested in much more. The fabric of

20. Hilary Weingarden, qtd. in Valenti, "Staring at Our Faces," para. 5.
21. Abrams, "Shutting Down Body Shame," para. 3.
22. Wiseman, "Amazing Grace Coddington," para. 15.

our character measures what is most important. Our physical and spiritual life need to be interwoven so we are "transformed by the renewing of [our minds]," as Rom 12:2 says. This is a sign of true godliness and Christian maturity. Proverbs 31:30 is spot on when it says, "Charm is deceitful, and beauty is fleeting: but a woman who fears the Lord is to be praised." This is a wonderful quote attributed to author Kate Angell: "Outer beauty attracts, but inner beauty captivates."[23] Our appearance does matter, but it is second to our soul. Our self-worth is not based on our looks. May God be our source of beauty!

Artistry in the Bible: A Reflection by Graham[24]

In this chapter, Jules wrote about the impact of Edith Schaeffer on her thinking about art and beauty. Interestingly, Francis Schaeffer, Edith's husband, had a similar impact on me. He authored a small book entitled *Art and the Bible*. It was an eye-opener for me. Schaeffer writes:

> The arts and the sciences do have a place in the Christian life—they are not peripheral. For a Christian, redeemed by the work of Christ and living within the norms of Scripture and under the leadership of the Holy Spirit, the Lordship of Christ should include an interest in the arts. A Christian should use these arts to the glory of God, not just as tracts, mind you, but as things of beauty to the praise of God. An artwork can be a doxology.[25]

How right Schaeffer is. We have permission to pursue the beautiful. Jules has done that with her fashion designs.

---

23. Kate Angell, qtd. in "46 Amazing Quotes," para. 23.

24. In this section, I focus on artistry and material creations. A wide-ranging treatment would look at music, drama, dance, architecture, and poetry in Scripture as well. The visual arts per se do not figure much in Scripture (e.g., painting), and this was probably due to the prohibitions on idolatry.

25. Schaeffer, *Art and the Bible*, 18.

The Bible, Beauty, and Clothing

God the Artist comes to the fore with the design of the tabernacle. According to Exod 25:9, God provided Moses with the pattern: "Make this tabernacle and all its furnishings exactly like the pattern I will show you." The tabernacle was a tent which was to be the dwelling place of God's glory as Israel journeyed through the wilderness. It housed sacred objects such as the tablets of the law, which were placed in an ark (a box made from wood), and a gold sculpture of a cherub (guardian angel) was placed at each end. To do the creative work, God raised up two artists. In Exod 31:1–9, we read how Bezalel and Oholiab (along with other skilled and intelligent workers) were especially chosen by God to work as artists/craftsmen to create beauty in the tabernacle. The workers, with their skilled intelligence and hands, crafted artistic designs from gold, silver, bronze, stone, and wood for God's people to enjoy. God had given them "wisdom, understanding and knowledge," and they were filled with the Spirit of God to carry out this creative task. In Exod 31:10, the Lord commanded that part of their artistic handiwork was to make "woven garments, both the sacred garments for Aaron the priest and garments for his sons when they serve[d] as priests."

The priestly garments for the tabernacle are especially interesting. Exodus 28:13 describes them in detail: "Make pomegranates of blue, purple and scarlet yarn around the hem of the robe, with gold bells between them." Francis Schaefer offers this insightful observation: "Purple and scarlet could be natural changes in the growth of pomegranates. But blue is not. The implication is that there is freedom to make something from nature but can be different from it and it too can be brought into the presence of God."[26] In other words, blue pomegranates are not found in nature. They are human artifacts. Nature is not simply being imitated. Artistic imagination is involved.

The later temple that Solomon built was even more striking than the tabernacle in artistry, scale, and beauty. Like the tabernacle, God is the Artist providing the pattern (1 Chron 28:11–13):

---

26. Schaeffer, *Art and the Bible*, 24.

> Then David gave his son Solomon the plans for the portico of the temple, its buildings, its storerooms, its upper parts, its inner rooms, and the place of atonement. He gave him the plans of all that the Spirit had put in his mind for the courts of the temple of the Lord and all the surrounding rooms, for the treasuries of the temple of God and for the treasuries for the dedicated things. He gave him instructions for the divisions of the priests and Levites and for all the work of serving in the temple of the Lord, as well as for all the articles to be used in its service.

The wall relief sculpture was particularly impressive: pomegranates, lilies, lions, oxen, cherubim, wreaths, palm trees, and flowers are mentioned (1 Kgs 7:13–50). In so many ways, this artwork was to create a sacred space reminiscent of the garden of God, Eden itself.[27]

Once more, Francis Schaeffer is insightful when he writes: "What, therefore, was to be in the temple? For one thing, the temple was to be filled with artwork."[28] Citing 2 Chr 3:6, he makes this key point: "Notice this carefully: The temple was covered with precious stones *for beauty*. There was no pragmatic reason for precious stones. They had no utilitarian purpose. God simply wanted beauty in the temple. God is interested in beauty."[29]

So much more could be written, but this brief treatment should indicate sufficiently that the God of the Bible is an artist and that human artistry can serve the purposes of God. And as we have seen regarding the priestly garments, clothing design was part of this Old Testament story.

---

27. Beale, "Eden," 15–16.
28. Schaeffer, *Art and the Bible*, 26.
29. Schaeffer, *Art and the Bible*, 26. Italics original.

Chapter 3

Fashion, Vanity, and Modesty

Adornment, what a science! Beauty, what a weapon!
Modesty, what elegance!

COCO CHANEL

Over the years I have learned that what is important
in a dress is the woman who is wearing it.

YVES SAINT-LAURENT

R<small>ECENTLY</small>, I was in a Bible study group with several other women. We sat around the table sipping coffee while watching a video presentation on 2 Corinthians by Beth Moore, an American evangelist, author, and Bible teacher. Once it was over, the leader asked, "Well, ladies, what did you think of the video?" The leader expected someone to share some deep spiritual insight about her message.

There was a long pause. So I spoke up: "Beth looked great in her *tight* striped pants, *well-cut* blouse, *trendy* short jacket, and *attractive* makeup. I think she looked fabulous!"

I am sure the leader and the other women were not expecting such a remark! I pointed out how her visual appearance was so pleasing that I sat up and listened to every word. A few days later over lunch, I was telling my beautiful Southern friend this story. She smiled and nodded. She had attended a function around the same time to hear a well-known women's speaker. Her experience was different than mine, but she identified with what I was saying. My friend went on to explain how jarring and distracting the speaker's style was. So much so that she could not listen to her talk. How interesting, I thought.

Our style does have a visual impact on others. Clothes communicate. They can attract, distract, convey authority, or be disempowering. Clothes influence how people view you and how you view others. It makes up 60–80 percent of all nonverbal communication. Never underestimate its importance!

The Outward and the Inward

Is looking stylish indulgent, frivolous, and worldly as a Christian? Is fashion only about vanity—i.e., a conceited concern with one's appearance—lust, and superficiality? Is applying makeup worldly? One day, I was chatting with a young woman at church. She was explaining her struggle to draw the line between desiring to express who God made her to be through her clothing/outward appearance and falling into vanity/materialism. Throwing money into the mix makes matters even more complicated, she said.

I believe we can dress creatively and in a stylish manner and wear makeup to enhance our facial appearance and skin tone. We can be into beauty as well as be devoted to God. Even so, fashion should not be an idol. Even good things such as sport and fitness can become an idol. We need to be aware that the Lord sees the attitude of our heart; therefore, we need to watch/pay attention to what we are most devoted to and what we set our eyes on.

As a Christian, I ask myself whether spending my time shopping and enjoying clothes is a waste of time and too worldly. Some years ago, I attended a dinner at my husband's divinity school, and

Fashion, Vanity, and Modesty

I was seated next to a woman I had not met before. So I introduced myself: "Hi, I'm Jules," I said.

"Hi, I'm Carol," she responded. So we continued chatting. "And what do you do for a living?" she asked. I know this always creates interest and an "Oh, how interesting" comment when I tell people I am a fashion designer! Most Christians have never met a Christian fashion designer. She then told me the story about her friend who had recently visited. She was feeling down and needed a change of scenery. To lift her spirits, they decided to go shopping. Carol's daughter, who loves clothes, did some online research for her mom's friend in preparation for their shopping trip. Carol mentioned how much fun they had shopping together. Then, in the next breath, she said how guilty her friend felt about spending money on clothes.

When thinking back on this conversation, it led me to reflect on the wise men bearing expensive gifts to give to a tiny child in a manger (Matt 2:11). After doing some research, I could see the deep meaning behind these costly gifts. First, gold was the metal for a king. This acknowledged his right to rule. Second, frankincense was used to anoint the priests of Israel. This significant gift was pointing to Christ as our great high priest. Last, myrrh was for embalmment, which was a symbol of Christ's death.[1] Were these gifts of gold, frankincense, and myrrh excessive and a waste of money? These gifts could have been sold for heaps of cash, and the money could have been given to the poor and needy. Matthew 26:6–13 tells of a woman who poured expensive perfume from a broken alabaster jar over Jesus' head. Perhaps you would question this extravagance, just as the disciples did. They asked, "Why this waste?" (Matt 26:8). Jesus did not think of it as such. He said, "She has done a beautiful thing to me. . . . When she poured this perfume on my body, she did it to prepare me for burial" (Matt 26:10–12). Could the money the woman spent on the expensive perfume have been put to better use? We could ask the same question about spending money on the clothing and makeup we buy.

---

1. Boice, "Gold, Incense, and Myrrh," para. 9.

However, think of Jesus' famous parable about the prodigal son returning home. The waiting father's reaction is instructive: "But the father said to his servants, 'Bring quickly the best robe, and put it on him, and put a ring on his hand, and shoes on his feet. And bring the fattened calf, kill it, and let us eat and celebrate. For this my son was dead, and is alive again; he was lost, and is found.' And they began to celebrate" (Luke 15:22–24). In the Bible, there are contexts and events where expense is fitting, and so, too, is celebrating in the best of garments.

Is there an advantage to dressing fashionably? Can we look our best to show that we care for ourselves? First, my research shows that wearing stylish clothes appropriately, such as in the office or law court, can make you more noticeable and help you to be taken more seriously. Therefore, a tailored pantsuit was an empowering style for women to wear in the '80s because it looked professional and polished. Second, having a unique, personal style can make you feel more confident about who you are. Third, dressing in a stylish way may inspire others. Fourth, when we dress appropriately, comfortably, and in a stylish manner, we can forget about ourselves and concentrate on others and more important matters.

Looking for stylish clothes that are God honoring can be challenging. Recently, I was looking at fashion from *Vogue* online. I saw some stylish outfits I could wear to the office, a party, or a special evening out. But then I saw some ugly, ridiculous-looking outfits which could only be worn on a catwalk. Fashion shows can be filled with unrealistic designs which would not be the preferred choice of the average woman. The shows are directed toward buyers (and celebrities), and often the garments are not practical to wear (especially when worn by skinny, tall models). These shows are a way to expose designers' collections and to represent their aesthetic and artisan craftsmanship (which, in many cases, can be beautiful). In some cases, a designer's values are put forward by the style of the clothes (e.g., cross-dressing styles and androgynous clothing). Of course, this is not the case for all designers. There are some designers who show us exciting and beautiful (and

Fashion, Vanity, and Modesty

expensive) clothes, such as Yves Saint Laurent, Prada, Carolina Herrera, and Gucci. Of course, realistically speaking, we are not going to love every piece of a designer's collection!

God does not judge us by our looks or by what we wear. We read in 1 Sam 16:7: "The Lord does not look at things people look at. People look at the outward appearance, but the Lord looks at the heart." Likewise, we are not to judge the value of others by how they look or by what they wear. Scripture backs this up when relating the story of how the Lord sent the prophet Samuel to Bethlehem to choose a new king from one of Jesse's sons. Each son paraded before Samuel, and they were rejected one by one because none of them was God's chosen one. The Lord tells Samuel that appearance and stature do not characterize the qualities of a good king. Then Jesse's eighth and youngest son, David, the shepherd boy, was displayed before Samuel. Even though David was ruggedly handsome, God did not choose him for his looks. He was chosen because of his upright character (1 Sam 16:1–13). James 2:1–7 also teaches us that whether someone joins the fellowship of your church wearing beautiful clothes or dressed in shabby, torn clothes, we are to treat them equally with respect. God does not want us to live in a discriminatory and judgmental way. We are not to treat people badly just because they look or dress a certain way. We are to live as little Christs in our actions. First John 3:18 encourages us to live this way: "Dear children, let us not love with words or tongue but with actions and in truth."

Vanity

In 1 Tim 2:9, the apostle Paul encourages women to "dress modestly, with decency and propriety, not with adorning hairstyles or gold or pearls or expensive clothes, but with good deeds, appropriate for women who profess to worship God." This verse is saying that beauty has to do with our character and not simply our outward appearance. God wants us to become beautiful on the inside—the kind of beauty that lasts forever. That kind of beauty shows itself in good deeds. Again, 1 Pet 3:3–4 tells us that a woman's true beauty should not come from her external beautification and adornment but from qualities such as humility and wholesomeness of her heart and mind. Peter does not forbid facials and beauty treatments or a new hair color. Neither is Peter banning the latest trendy color of lipstick! Rather, the beauty he is writing about comes from "your inner self, the unfading beauty of a gentle and quiet spirit" (1 Pet 3:4). Once again, we see the Bible's emphasis on and valuing of the inward rather than the outward.

Above all, Scripture encourages us to understand that in God's sight, our true beauty comes from our character. Proverbs 31:30 makes this point: "Charm is deceptive, and beauty fleeting: but a woman who fears the Lord is to be praised."

Context and Costume

Danielle Peterson Searls summarizes the thought of Roland Barthes, a French literary theorist, philosopher, and critic: "Fashion is not only clothes and accessories, but also a language that harmonizes with a time and place. Along with the obvious reason clothing was invented—'as protection against harsh weather, out of modesty for hiding nudity, and for ornamentation to get noticed'—Barthes says that fashion serves another essential function: storytelling."[2]

It is important to dress in context. There is a difference between our clothing and a costume. Our clothing is like a second skin. A costume that you would wear for Halloween lets us dress up to project another character. We need to ask ourselves if a certain outfit is appropriate for the occasion and place. For example, kilts for men in Scotland, a swimsuit/bikini at Bondi Beach (Australia) or Cancún (Mexico), and a short tennis skirt/dress worn at Wimbledon. Recently, I was having dinner with some friends. They asked me about this book, which we were in the process of writing at the time. We got into discussing the topic of modesty. One of my friends then told me how a young woman one Sunday

---

2. Searls, "Crusader Chic," para. 1.

Fashion, Vanity, and Modesty

at her church was dressed in booty shorts. My friend said that as she walked forward for Communion, she could not take her eyes off her because there was too much skin showing off her buttocks and she felt distracted. I am not condemning wearing booty shorts, but were they worn in context on this occasion? In the same way, a bikini would not be appropriate to wear for a church worship service. Today, there is fluidity when it comes to fashion. Perhaps some people do not care about dressing appropriately for the context or place.

As women, we are responsible for how we dress and for doing so in context for each setting. It was no different for women believers in Greco-Roman society to dress in context to suit their situation. We read in 1 Cor 11:6: "For if a woman does not cover her head, she might as well have her hair cut off; but if it is a disgrace for a woman to have her hair cut off or her head shaved, then she should cover her head." The church had a serious dress code for women regarding hair covering. Why was the covering/uncovering of a woman's head such a hot issue in the Corinthian church? To understand this, the cultural context needs to be considered. Only prostitutes and dancing girls let their hair down in public. Married women, on the other hand, were required to wear a head covering or decorative headband in public. At home, amongst family and friends, she could let her hair down! If formal guests arrived, she would modestly pull a scarf-like piece of cloth (which was draped over her shoulders) over her head. It seems that women believers in the Corinthian church found the rule confusing, because they were uncertain if the church gathering (most likely held in a home) was public or private.[3] Paul considered church gatherings as community events. In this case, Paul's counsel was that every woman who prophesied or prayed was to have her head covered. The head covering showed respect to her husband as a married woman. Hence, this is how married women were to dress within the Corinthian church.

In the fundamentalist church I attended in my youth, every female—child, teenager, or mature woman—was required to wear

---

3. Instone-Brewer, *Moral Questions*, 239–41.

a head covering because of this text in 1 Corinthians! The strict head-covering rule could not be broken, because we were sitting before the King of kings and in the presence of male members. So, the reading of this controversial verse was not read in context, and the surrounding conditions were not considered. Nevertheless, as a young fashionista, I enjoyed the parade of stylish designer hats worn each Sunday.

Modesty

A friend told me the following amusing story. Her husband, as a young college student, was given this advice by his professor about writing an essay: "An essay is like a miniskirt—short enough to keep interest and long enough to cover everything important."

Modesty refers to what people feel is the proper way for clothing to cover the body. Modesty avoids indecency and impropriety in dress. Modesty is also about privacy. These are wise words attributed to Marilyn Monroe: "Our clothes should be tight enough to show you're a woman, but loose enough to show you're a lady."[4] We need to be conscious and alert to the message and values we communicate by what we wear. Without a doubt, wearing sexually provocative clothing is sending a certain message. I share another quote with you, this one anonymous: "Showing a great amount of skin when you dress up isn't the way to find prince charming. Prince charming likes his gifts wrapped."[5]

We were born stark naked, so why do we need to be modest? Isn't it natural to be uncovered? In Genesis, we find Adam and Eve naked in the lush garden of Eden, which God provided for them to enjoy. They felt no shame, guilt, or embarrassment. They were innocent and open in their nakedness (Gen 2:25). They were free to eat from any tree in the garden except from the tree in the middle of the garden (Gen 3:2). Then they blew it! The alluring, crafty serpent tempted them to eat fruit from the tree which God

---

4. Marilyn Monroe, qtd. in "Classy Women Sayings," para. 9.
5. "Classy Women," para. 8.

Fashion, Vanity, and Modesty

had forbidden. They fell for the serpent's deception and ate the fruit because it was so pleasing to the eyes! The consequence of Adam and Eve's sin was that they felt ashamed and self-conscious in their nakedness. Subsequently, they hid amongst the trees of the garden because they felt guilty and exposed before a holy God. God heard them among the rustling trees and asked them why they were hiding. Adam's response in Gen 3:10 is telling: "I was afraid because I was naked . . ." From this time on, nudity became problematic, and the need for modesty and a covering was set in motion! It must be noted that Adam and Eve's nudity and shame has far more significance for us, which is aptly illustrated in the *Dictionary of Biblical Imagery*: "Being unclothed thus becomes a metaphor for being exposed to the judgment of God."[6] Hebrews 4:13 tells us, "Everything is uncovered and laid bare before the eyes of him to whom we must give account." Also, in Jer 23:24, the Lord declares, "Can a man hide in secret places where I cannot see him? Do I not fill the heavens and earth?"

Why do some women show off their bodies? Is it self-seeking or to attract attention? Or is it to empower themselves and gain confidence? Is it a form of self-expression? Perhaps some women feel less beautiful and less confident when they do not expose their bodies. Maybe it is to impress other women or to find a sexual partner. We live in such a sexualized culture, which drives marketing, media, and entertainment. The world tells us we need to look pretty, appealing, and sexy to be valued. The fashion industry markets sexy clothes to communicate that "sexy" will make women feel more attractive. At the time of writing this chapter, there are many sexual-abuse cases. Actors, politicians, TV personalities, and even pastors are being prosecuted for their abusive sexual behavior! As Christians, we have a responsibility to dress in a way that is God honoring. We are told in Scripture to control our desires, as our body is the temple of the Holy Spirit (1 Cor 6:12–20). Indeed, this goes for anything that becomes an obsession—whether it is sex, alcohol, or overeating. The apostle Paul drives the application home: "So glorify God in your body" (1 Cor 6:20).

6. Ryken et al., *Dictionary of Biblical Imagery*, 582.

We hope to shed some insight and wisdom into the topic of modesty to help us be more thoughtful about our clothing choices. One person may think a slit in a skirt up to the thigh is appropriate. Another person may feel it is inappropriate to show their belly but feels comfortable wearing a low neckline. I am not about to lay down the law about modestly restrictions. Some women believe that being provocatively dressed is cool, cute, fashionable, and alluring. They do not realize it can be viewed as an invitation for sexual advances. They do not think about the impact it has on others, and especially on the other sex. These are powerful words from the Apocrypha: "Avert your eyes from a shapely woman: do not gaze upon beauty that is not yours; through woman's beauty many have been ruined, for love of it burns like fire."[7] I believe there is a connection between our heart and our eyes. Job's words are wise. He made this promise: "I made a covenant with my eyes not to look lustfully at a young woman" (Job 31:1). He did not let his heart be led by his eyes.

It can be hard to find suitable clothing when your desire is to honor God with how you dress. We will never all agree on every clothing item when it comes to modesty. When it comes to modesty standards of what is decent and socially acceptable, it differs between people and cultures. Muslim culture demands modesty. Women of Islamic faith are expected to cover their bodies and hair by wearing a burka. In Sudan in 2014, nine women were punished for wearing Western-style pants. They received forty lashes for this offence. In Saudi Arabia, whether you are a local girl or a foreigner, showing an inch of skin is illegal. In Uganda, if you are caught wearing a skirt or shorts above the knee, you face an arrest.[8] As we can see, modesty is contextual and must be culturally appropriate.

As followers of Christ, the question needs to be asked: How is "modest" being defined? Recently, I was listening to country radio, and a line from the song "I Lived It" by Blake Shelton caught my

---

7. Ben Sira 9:8. The Apocrypha contains books not in our canon of Scripture, and so it must be read carefully. Even so, there is wisdom in the apocryphal books in a number of places.

8. Bruce-Lockhart, "5 Countries," para. 8.

Fashion, Vanity, and Modesty

attention. It mentioned someone wearing a skirt to church that was not long enough. The subtitle of this book asks, "How high is a holy hemline?" The purpose of this chapter is not to present a prescriptive Christian dress code on what we should or should not wear. Modestly is open to different interpretations. Perhaps we need something between wearing a burka and being half naked. You need to decide what you are going to cover up and what you want to show. We suggest asking this question when looking at someone: Where do my eyes go? Is it to the *whole* person? Or is it the neckline revealing deep cleavage or to the thigh exposed by a short hemline?

Recently, I saw a picture of a friend's daughter's wedding dress. Her daughter was voluptuous, and the low neckline accentuated her large breasts. As a female, my eyes went straight to the cleavage. As I looked at her photo, her breasts were the focal point. On my first glimpse, I did not see her beautiful face or the delicate lace of the dress because I was distracted by too much skin. I did not see the beauty of the whole person. When relating this story to a friend, she told me a similar tale of a dress worn by a violinist sitting center stage in an orchestra. Her evening gown had a one-sided, thigh-high split. The way she sat accentuated her leg. My friend said her eyes went straight to the violinist's thigh, which was the focal point of the person. My friend was totally distracted from hearing the beautiful music. I like what the designer Diane von Fürstenburg said: "It's the woman you should remember, not the dress, ever."[9] When we look at how someone is dressed, surely we want to see the *whole* person and not be distracted by a part of the body. In 2015, the organizers of Christian Fashion Week sought to express a biblical Christian worldview. When choosing the designer lineup, their goal was to model modesty. Executive director Jose Gomez explained:

> The designers that we have chosen for The Final Season represent a wide spectrum of choices available for men and women who hold modesty as a core value. . . . However, what is of more significance is the fact that

9. Fürstenburg, "It's the Woman . . ."

each brand in our showcase has also paid special attention to environmental and human rights concerns. There is a culture of sustainability as well as social and environmental responsibility that counts for much more than regulating hemlines and cleavage.[10]

A non-Christian approach says, "My body is my own. I will do whatever I like with it. I'll wear whatever I like." In contrast, 1 Cor 6:13 tells us that "the body is not meant for sexual immorality but for the Lord, and the Lord for the body." This verse clearly states that our body is the temple of the Holy Spirit. For this reason, we need to care for and honor our bodies, as our body does not belong to us. It belongs to God and is sacred. Yes, our bodies can be celebrated because God made us. It is important to appreciate our body and treat it well, because it glorifies God. We *do* need to be body conscious, but not self-conscious. If we destroy our body, we destroy the temple of God.

Being fully covered can also be provocative and revealing of the female form. For example, when women wear leggings, you are fully covered. Yet, they can be revealing because they are tightly fitted. There is nothing wrong with leggings. In fact, they are amazingly comfortable for working out and for everyday wear, but they are shape revealing. One can also wear a high-neck, ankle-length dress. Even though the body is fully covered, provocatively placed, sheer fabric sections rob the garment of modesty. On the other hand, a bikini might show more skin but may not be as provocative and revealing.

Another part of modesty is doing the "lean-forward test" to see what you may be exposing. I recall going to an eye doctor's appointment some years ago. I was surprised by how the receptionist was dressed. As she sat at her desk, I leaned over to make my appointment. All I could see were her large breasts bulging out of her dress. She had not done the "lean-forward test." I felt awkward as a woman and needed to avert my eyes! Was this appropriate dress for the place and occasion? I also remember eating in a restaurant in Denver, Colorado. The cute little waitress serving

10. "Christian Fashion Week," para. 2.

us wore a super-short skirt. As we observed her, she was tugging the length of her skirt downward as she walked between customers trying to balance her drink tray. She was obviously extremely uncomfortable.

One year, I read a helpful Advent series written by the New Testament scholar Tom Wright. His comment on Matt 6:16–24, which addresses fasting and lasting treasure, stood out to me because of its relevancy to modesty:

> I think Jesus literally meant that we should take care of what we actually look at. Where do your eyes naturally get drawn to? Are you in control of them, or do they take you—and your mind and heart—wherever they want? . . . The eyes are like headlights of a car. Supposing you're driving along a dark road at night and you switch the lights on—and nothing happens! You suddenly realize just how dark it really is. That's what it's like, Jesus is saying, if your eyes are not on God, and if instead they are following whatever eye-catching, pretty thing happens to take their fancy. Priorities again. Are your eyes leading you in the right direction showing you the road ahead?[11]

What catches our attention says a lot about us, for good or ill.

Finally, be aware of how you dress. Be respectful. Ask yourself, "How does my clothing impact those around me?" It is possible to dress modestly and look stylish. Jackie O is an example of a woman of class who always dressed modestly and elegantly and looked beautiful. Above all, remember that Scripture makes it clear that beauty does not start on the outside but rather starts from within. Coco Chanel wisely said, "Adornment, what a science! Beauty, what a weapon! Modesty, what elegance!"[12]

---

11. Wright, *Advent for Everyone*, 103–4.
12. Chanel, "Adornment, What a Science!" 33.

Faith and Fashion

How High Is a Holy Hemline? A Reflection by Graham

"How high is a holy hemline?" is the subtitle of this book. It is a question that raises the issue of modesty. Jules has addressed the modesty question in this chapter in several ways. I want to draw attention to some complementary perspectives.

In the Bible, modesty is about restraint as opposed to ostentatious self-display.[13] Modesty is the opposite in attitude to "Look at me, look at me!" Vanity is not a Christian option. Self-display in clothing can also distract the onlooker. Here is the advice for attendees from one church that is aware of the distraction problem: "We believe that the Bible isn't specifically concerned about how we look on the outside or about the clothes we wear when we worship God. Some people prefer to dress more formally as a symbol of respect. But generally the guideline is to be sensible and wear clothes that will not distract others."[14]

The apostle Paul offers counsel on female adornment. My guess is that how some women were adorning themselves created pastoral issues for Paul which he needed to address. Paul writes to his younger associate Timothy about congregational life: "I . . . want the women to dress modestly, with decency and propriety, adorning themselves, not with elaborate hairstyles or gold or pearls or expensive clothes, but with good deeds, appropriate for women who profess to worship God" (1 Tim 2:9–10). Did such dress and such accessories create distractions in corporate worship? This is a view many commentators hold, as Philip Towner acknowledges.[15] He also suggests a further possibility: "But perhaps the more acute problem was that of insensitive women flaunting their dress, jewelry and hairstyles in a way that hurt the feelings of the poorer members of the church." Towner adds, "The kinds of adornments

---

13. Field, "Modesty," 599.
14. "Frequently Asked Questions," para. 6.
15. Towner, *1–2 Timothy & Titus*, comment on 1 Tim 2:8–9.

Fashion, Vanity, and Modesty

mentioned (*braided hair ... gold ... pearls ... expensive clothes*) all belonged to that culture's critical caricature of wealthy women."[16]

The apostle Peter also offers counsel on the matter of adornment. Peter's purpose seems different than Paul's, as he addresses matters concerning husbands and wives, especially pagan spouses. Addressing wives, he writes: "Do not let your adorning be external—the braiding of hair and the putting on of gold jewelry, or the clothing you wear—but let your adorning be the hidden person of the heart with the imperishable beauty of a gentle and quiet spirit, which in God's sight is very precious" (1 Pet 3:3–4). Peter draws attention to the distinction between the inner and the outer. As I. Howard Marshall comments: "The desire for outward beauty can easily lead to the sins of pride and vanity as well as the wrong use of money."[17] Even so, Peter's instruction to wives should not be misunderstood. E. P. Clowney wisely comments on the story of the prodigal son: "The point is not a legalistic ban on beauty of attire. ... The point is the vastly superior value of inward beauty and the danger of extravagant and sensual fashions in dress."[18]

Figures of the early church such as Cyprian, bishop of Carthage (martyred 258 AD), took Paul's and Peter's apostolic instruction with utmost seriousness. He addresses the wealthy women in a forceful way: "You call yourself wealthy and rich; but Paul [he quotes 1 Tim 2:9–10] meets your riches, and with his own voice prescribes for the moderating of your dress and ornament within a just limit."[19] Cyprian argues that Peter similarly called for restraint in dressing up.[20] New Testament scholar David Instone-Brewer points out that the rich in Roman society "spent huge amounts on their appearance."[21] That was also the case in Cyprian's day. There is another cultural fact that is true about both New Testament

---

16. Towner, *1–2 Timothy & Titus*, comment on 1 Tim 2:8–9. Italics in the original.
17. Marshall, *1 Peter*, comment on 1 Pet 3:2–6.
18. Clowney, *Message of 1 Peter*, 131.
19. Cyprian of Carthage, "Treatise 2," ch. 2, para. 8.
20. Cyprian of Carthage, "Treatise 2," ch. 2, para. 8.
21. Instone-Brewer, *Moral Questions*, 239.

times and Cyprian's third-century setting: the women who dressed ostentatiously and immodestly tended to be the prostitutes.[22]

Instone-Brewer has further insight to offer on the matter of dress. He writes: "What concerned Peter and Paul mostly were displays of ostentatious wealth that included wearing expensive jewelry, clothes and hairstyles. As well as demonstrating a worldly concern with outward beauty rather than inner holiness, this showed these women had little concern for the poor and needy."[23] He elaborates by applying Paul's and Peter's counsel to our world: "If the apostles were addressing today's church, they might have included warning about flashy cars, trophy wives, and homes filled with the latest high-tech gizmos. . . . Peter and Paul were criticizing all types of selfish squandering. It's a message that urges us to makes sure we remember where our real treasure is."[24]

So how high is a holy hemline? It is easier to say what it is not. As Jules argued earlier in this chapter, if the hemline is where one's eye goes first rather than to the whole person or the person's face, that may be the clue to recognizing a hemline that is too high or, for that matter, a neckline that is too low.

---

22. "The characteristics of ornaments, and of garments, and the allurements of beauty, are not fitting for any but prostitutes and immodest women" (Cyprian of Carthage, "Treatise 2," para. 12). Tertullian (c. 160–225 AD) wrote an entire treatise on the subject of women's dress and ornamentation. Some of it is quite bizarre. For example, he argued that women's ornamentation came from fallen angels. But to Tertullian's credit, he also had a chapter on the need for men to be modest in dress and ornamentation (see Tertullian, "On the Apparel").

23. Instone-Brewer, *Moral Questions*, 243.

24. Instone-Brewer, *Moral Questions*, 243–44.

Chapter 4

Wardrobe Wisdom

> I think our bodies are beautiful, and I think celebrating them and being comfortable in them—no matter what age you are—is important. There shouldn't be any kind of shame or discomfort around it.
>
> JENNIFER ANISTON

> The best color in the whole world is the one that looks good on you.
>
> COCO CHANEL

AMERICAN singer-songwriter Miranda Lambert has had quite a journey accepting who she is when looking at herself in the mirror:

> I've been all sizes. My whole life, I have struggled with ups and downs in weight. . . . I'm only 5'4" so weight shows quickly on me. . . . [I've now] hit a comfortable place. . . . It's so good to find your place. I don't like being onstage worrying about my body. That's the last

thing I want to be thinking about. I don't give my best performance when I'm distracted by my insecurities.[1]

Many of us find it hard to accept our bodies, and we feel especially insecure in what we wear. The expectations are that we need to be slim, pretty, and have a great body. It must be pointed out that being attractive, skinny, and model-like does not necessarily bring happiness! They have their body-image problems too. Owning beautiful clothing and looking thin and slender will never satisfy our soul or give us God's peace.

These are wise words attributed to the famous novelist J. K. Rowling:

> "Fat" is usually the first insult a girl throws at another girl when she wants to hurt her.
>
> I mean, is "fat" really the worst thing a human being can be? Is "fat" worse than "vindictive," "jealous," "shallow," "vain," "boring" or "cruel"? Not to me; but then, you might retort, what do I know about the pressure to be skinny? I'm not in the business of being judged on my looks, what with being a writer and earning my living by using my brain . . .
>
> I went to the British Book Awards that evening. After the award ceremony I bumped into a woman I hadn't seen for nearly three years. The first thing she said to me? "You've lost a lot of weight since the last time I saw you!"
>
> "Well," I said, slightly nonplussed, "the last time you saw me I'd just had a baby."
>
> What I felt like saying was, "I've produced my third child and my sixth novel since I last saw you. Aren't either of those things more important, more interesting, than my size?" But no—my waist looked smaller! Forget the kid and the book: finally, something to celebrate!
>
> I've got two daughters who will have to make their way in this skinny-obsessed world, and it worries me, because I don't want them to be empty-headed, self-obsessed, emaciated clones; I'd rather they were

---

1. Taylor, "Miranda Lambert," paras. 2–4.

Wardrobe Wisdom

independent, interesting, idealistic, kind, opinionated, original, funny—a thousand things, before "thin."[2]

Most women do not have ideal "fashion-model" bodies. In the 1950s, the "ideal figure" concentrated on curves. Think Marilyn Munroe and Elizabeth Taylor. Weight was not the focus, but having a slim waist was. Then, in the rock-and-rolling 1960s and 1970s, the stick-thin model type figure—think Twiggy—was popular. Since 2020, on the rise is the Kardashian body type—big bust and buttocks and flat stomach. For some these days, an ideal body shape can only be formed through surgery. How sad!

A biblical theology of your physical body is not normally a hot-topic sermon you hear in church. Yet, despite this, the Bible has much to say about the body. A good body image starts with believing and understanding how God views us. To do this, you need a good sense of self and acceptance of how God created you. The psalmist in Ps 139:13–16 tells us that we are fearfully and wonderfully made by God our Creator:

> For you created my inmost being;
>   you knit me together in my mother's womb.
> I praise you because I am fearfully and wonderfully made;
>   your works are wonderful,
>   I know that full well.
> My frame was not hidden from you
>   when I was made in the secret place,
>   when I was woven together in the depths of the earth.
> Your eyes saw my unformed body;
>   all the days ordained for me were written in your book
>   before one of them came to be.

We are all imperfect, as a quote attributed to author Brene Brown says: "You are imperfect, you are wired for struggle, but you are worthy of love and belonging."[3] The biblical picture, more importantly, tells us that it's God's love for us that gives us ultimate value and worth. God does not look at our body dimensions, our skin color, or our imperfections and offer a value judgment on them.

2. Rowling, "'Fat' Is Usually . . ."
3. Brown, "You Are Imperfect . . ."

Instead, we can confidently be sure of God's unconditional love for us. In the Old Testament, we read in Jer 31:3: "I have loved you with an everlasting love..." And in the New Testament, 1 John 3:1: "See what great love the Father has lavished on us, that we should be called children of God!"

I have spent a lot of time fitting women's bodies in my work as a designer. When creating garments for customers, I have found very few women who are satisfied with their bodies. Many women feel shame about their bodies. It was revealing to read a PsychAlive article citing a survey showing that "97 percent of women questioned had an 'I hate my body' thought on an average day."[4]

With access to images on social media and with an emphasis on body image, we can take on unrealistic beauty standards. Industries exist to make you feel dissatisfied with your bodies because so much emphasis is placed on how you should look. Aspects of our culture (e.g., media, Hollywood, and glossy magazines) can influence us to pay too much unrealistic attention to our bodies, and so we may worry about our body image and how others see us. This can make us feel dissatisfied with our body and self-conscious about how we look. Yet, God does not see us this way, and what God thinks about you matters most. God loves you, thinks you're special, and values you. Knowing who you are in God's sight means you can walk out the door feeling confident, knowing you are loved and precious no matter how you dress. In fact, the opinions of others do not matter.

We may look at others and what they own in general and what they wear. We can be anxious that we simply do not measure up. Instead, focus on what your God-given body can do. Your heart beats, the human brain has memory capacity, your muscles allow movement to walk and run, and your hands allow you to write, carry things, and text on your phone! A quote attributed to writer and blogger Jess C. Scotto sums this up so well: "The human body is the best work of art."[5] This is such an important claim, but how

---

4. PsychAlive, "I Hate My Body," para. 1.
5. Scott, "The Human Body..."

much of the Bible backs it up? Happily, the Bible makes it crystal clear that we matter to God. God values and loves us.

We will have days when we feel unhappy about our body image and imperfections. It may be because you have eaten too much chocolate—or, if you're like me, too much left-over Pavlova (a meringue Aussie dessert) after a dinner party. Amy Bloom, an American writer and psychotherapist, is credited for saying, "You are imperfect, permanently and inevitably flawed. And you are beautiful."[6] Even though you may well believe that God accepts you and loves you as you are, you may still struggle with low self-esteem and have negative thought patterns related to your body image. We all need to accept the fact that we have imperfections!

God does care about what you think about your body. It is important to see your body not as your own but as the temple of the Holy Spirit, as 1 Cor 6:19–20 tells us: "Do you not know that your bodies are temples of the Holy Spirit, who is in you, whom you have received from God? You are not your own, you were bought with a price. Therefore, honor God with your bodies." God wants us to treat our bodies well and to cherish them. Part of honoring and caring for our bodies may involve physical exercise, following a healthy eating plan, and controlling our sexual desires. Our overarching outlook should be one of loving, honoring, and caring for our bodies as a work in progress toward body positivity and not body shame.

Be encouraged by what Allison Abrams, licensed psychotherapist in New York City, has said, "Hopefully, with continued movements toward body positivity, the trend will begin to shift from body-shaming to celebrating women of all sizes, shapes, colors, and bra sizes."[7] A good body image is set in motion by having a good sense of self and acceptance of how God created you. When you do this, you can dress to suit *your* body shape.

---

6. Bloom, "You Are Imperfect . . ."
7. Abrams, "Shutting Down Body Shame," para. 11.

Faith and Fashion

Dress to Your Body Shape: Fit Matters

When styling yourself, the first and most important thing is to understand your body shape. Body shape refers to three defining points: bust, waist, and hips. Body shapes are diverse. There are many body shapes, such as rectangle, oval, hourglass, triangle, and inverted triangle. Each body shape needs to be treated with respect and dignity, because we are all fearfully and wonderfully made by God, our Creator (Ps 139:14). Therefore, God has not created one body shape better than another.

In preparation for this book, I read many articles about style, trends, and fashion in general. One common thread was emphasized repeatedly. Fit matters. You may ask, "Is fit really that important?" For one, garments that fit well last longer. Second, garments that are too tight can tear away at the seams more easily. Third, garments that are too loose hang on the body improperly. Many people are unaware of how a garment should fit individual body shapes, and perhaps they are not even interested! Fit is about the cut of a garment. It is not about the material the garment is cut from and stitched in. The cut is about the style and shape of the garment and how it hangs on your body.

Garments come in different fit categories: fitted, relaxed fit, and oversized fit. What makes the difference between each fit category is called "wearing ease." These are the extra inches/centimeters of fabric volume incorporated into the cut of the garment for design purposes and so you move freely for daily activities and feel comfortable. For example, only an inch or two of wearing ease is added to a fitted garment. In contrast, an oversized garment may have up to ten or more inches of wearing ease. Because of this phenomenon, you may wear varying sizes. For example, in an oversized style, you may actually be the right size, or you may need to downsize. Then, if the garment you are purchasing has a tight fit, you may need to size up. Depending on which body shape you are (rectangle, oval, hourglass, triangle, or inverted triangle), some cuts, and silhouettes will suit you better than others.[8]

---

8. The silhouette is the outline that creates the overall shape and volume

Wardrobe Wisdom

Fit is one of the most important aspects of looking good because it affects your appearance. Cristóbal Balenciaga was an expert at fitting female bodies. In the 1960s, his masterpieces of sculptural purity lifted his work into the arena of art. His cut was legendary. Nothing fitted the body with the supple ease of a Balenciaga suit, and once women had worn his clothes, they were often unwilling to wear anything else.[9] I understand why Grace Kelly and Jackie Kennedy wore his gowns. I'm sure they would have felt extremely at ease, relaxed, and comfortable wearing such luxury.

When looking for clothes, you do not need to squeeze into a particular size of dress. Today, designers define sizes by their own preferences. Even the same designer's sizing can differ each season. This makes it very frustrating for shoppers because of sizing confusion. In one brand, you may be size eight, and in another size ten. Even size-ten clothes from a variety of designers can fit differently. If a garment feels tight and restricting, put it back on the rack! Then look at the next size up. Focus on buying the size that fits your fullest curves and feels most comfortable. Take no notice of the size number of the clothing. Do not stress if you need to wear a size up in a certain brand.

Be mindful too that as you age, a woman's body shape will change, so you need to adapt to this reality. Mass-produced, ready-to-wear clothes have a generic fit for the average woman, so it is very possible that for some individuals, the clothing will be ill-fitting in certain places. For this reason, many ready-to-wear styles may need to be altered to fit your shape. If you are between sizes, buy the bigger size and pay a tailor or alteration specialist to perfect the fit. It will make an enormous difference in how the garment looks and feels when it fits your body curves. In contrast, custom-made garments are made-to-measure and shaped to fit uniquely to an individual's body frame. In this case, it is easier to match design aesthetic to body shape. This method of constructing a garment solves the problem of unusual body dimensions because

of a garment. Part of the silhouette is the neckline and armhole shape, hem length, skirt shape and sleeve length.

9. "Introducing Cristóbal Balenciaga," para. 9.

the garment is made to fit each curve seamlessly. Before the garment is created, measurements must be taken. The measurements are then transformed into paper patterns. A toile or muslin is then constructed and modified. After these steps, the garment is cut and constructed in the final fabric.[10]

Too many women try to camouflage their body size/weight under their clothes. It is a myth to think that wearing loose-fitting, oversized tops and dresses will camouflage figure challenges. Wearing clothing that are too big will make you look heavier! There are better ways to mask some challenging body shapes. An important part of achieving a great body shape in your clothes is wearing proper foundation garments. It is essential to wear a well-fitted, uplifting bra. A body shaper will elevate how the garment looks when it comes to the fit. A body shaper creates a smooth, svelte silhouette, especially when wearing evening wear and knit garments. So, before you discern the fit of any garment, make sure you are wearing the "right" foundation garments. Was the actress Melissa McCarthy from the cast of *Nine Perfect Strangers* wearing great foundation garments for her plus-size body in the series? Perhaps so. Even at the height of 5'2", she totally rocked it in her beautifully fitted outfits shaped to her sizable frame. The actress demonstrates how a larger person can wear fitted clothes.

The fit of a garment is so important and should not be underestimated. No matter what your body type or favorite garment fit is, it is essential that the garment is secured to the body in certain areas. For tops and dresses, it is the neckline and shoulder area. For pants and skirts, it is the waistline. The waistline should fit snuggly but not too tight. If this is not the case, the garment will feel uncomfortable to wear. If a garment fits you poorly (too tight/loose or with a gaping neckline/armhole), it will be noticed! You will also feel uncomfortable wearing it. If your clothing fits well and feels comfortable, you can walk out the door feeling confident and ready to embrace the world, forgetting about yourself and not having to worry how your clothing looks.

---

10. A toile or muslin is an initial version of a garment made in cheap fabric to test the fit and design.

Wardrobe Wisdom

To develop an "eye" for a good fit, learn how to read the fabric signs of a bad fit in these areas:

Dresses, Tops, and Jackets

- Front shirt gaping when buttoned indicates it is too tight!
- Diagonal pull lines pointing from underarm up to sleeve cap (top point of sleeve on the shoulder) indicates that the sleeve does not have sufficient length from underarm to sleeve cap.
- A gaping neckline is caused by a garment that is too big across the chest—you will be pulling at it all the time to adjust it.
- A strapless dress or top that must be pulled up or constantly readjusted does not fit correctly. Strapless garments *must* be structured with boning to stay put on the body.
- On dresses, jackets, and coats, drooping shoulders are ill-fitting—unless it is a dropped shoulder line. The shoulder line should sit on the outer tips of your shoulders. Coco Chanel said, "A beautiful dress may look beautiful on the hanger, but it must be seen on the shoulders, with the movement of the arms and legs and the waist."[11]
- The bust darts in a top, dress, or jacket are the most important aspect to creating a smooth, flattering fit. It is one of the hardest to fit because it is dependent on the cup size and placement of a woman's breast on the body. Horizontal bust darts from the side seam or vertical bust darts from the hip to the bust must end slightly back from the center point of each breast (this is called "the apex"). When the bust-dart intake is not enough for your cup size, the garment will form folds under the arm on the side seam.[12]
- A dress with a waistline that forms a fold above the waist is too long from shoulder to the waist.

11. Grant, *Pocket Coco Chanel Wisdom*, 18.
12. The bust-dart intake is added at the pattern-making stag; therefore, after the garment is made, it is difficult to alter.

- A jacket that is too tight (when buttoned) on the hips will cause the jacket to form a fold (or bulge) around the waistline. When buying a top or jacket, button it up—give yourself a big hug with both arms to make sure there is adequate room in the garment. Also, a back vent in a jacket will allow for more freedom of movement when working in the office or getting in and out of a car.
- A long sleeve draping over your hand is too long.
- An ultrawide sleeve on a jacket broadens the arm.
- A sleeve that is too tight will not allow you to comfortably bend your arms or reach upward with ease.

Pants and Skirts

- An uncomfortable waistband when sitting is too tight.
- A garment too tight can cause a stressed zipper.
- Ideally, the garment should fit smoothly over the hips and buttocks when zippered or buttoned, without wrinkling or pulling. Make sure you have enough room in the hips to feel comfortable when sitting and bending.
- Horizontal creases across the hip area of pants (or a skirt) indicate that the garment is too tight.
- The back of pants cutting between the buttocks indicates that the rise (length from waist to crotch) is too short.
- A front smiley crotch crease indicates that the crotch length is too short.
- A sagging crotch indicates that crotch to waist is too long.
- Vertical folds of excess fabric form if pants or skirts are too big across the hips.
- The length of pants and skirts varies from fashion year to fashion year—discern what suits you best. A hemline finishing on the heaviest part of legs can add pounds—check how

your knees look when wearing a miniskirt, because knees are not the most flattering body part.

Seeking the expertise of an alteration specialist can be helpful in fitting your clothes to your individual shape. For example, nipping in the waist, stitching darts to create shape, taking up the shoulders, taking in the hips, etc., can make an enormous change in how the garment fits. If you buy a size up, most fitting issues can be fixed. Do be aware that a garment too small or too tight for you can be difficult to alter.

How, then, do you dress in a stylish, age-appropriate way? First, learning what are the best styles, cut, and fit of garments for you becomes particularly important. I have two friends who connect with certain brands because the style, cut, and fit suit their body type and age group. They shop these go-to brands when they need a top, jacket, or pants. This is wisdom. Take a good look at the quality of your skin and body shape before deciding whether you are wearing an age-appropriate, put-together outfit; also ask the opinion of a good friend. Some people would never wear skinny jeans because of the tight-fit cut. It may not suit their body type or frame. Yet, for me as a mature woman, I can wear them because they suit my body shape. How I create my "look" wearing skinny jeans differs from how my daughter creates her "look" when wearing skinny jeans. Age makes a difference.

Proportion and Balance is Key

When the designer Carolina Herrera was asked what fashion is all about, she said, "Proportion. It has to be perfect."[13] Coco Chanel also said, "Fashion is architecture: it is a matter of proportions."[14] Both designers understand the significance of proportion. Proportion is how your various body parts relate to one another. It is the relationship of your upper body to your lower body, the length of your torso and legs, as well as the position of your waistline.

13. Martin, "Carolina Herrera," 8.
14. Grant, *Pocket Coco Chanel Wisdom*, 16.

We are all unique and proportioned differently! Some people are tall, some petite, some rounded, some curvier in the hips, some straight up and down, some broad or narrow in the shoulders. There is no normal or typical body shape.

No matter what your body type, the aim is to balance the distance across the shoulders with the hips/thighs by using proportional balance and scale. Let me give example of how this can be so effective. I recently fitted a woman for her full-length, mother-of-the-bride dress. She had a heavy frame, with hips wider than her shoulders. She was styled with an empire-waist dress, V-neckline, and flared skirt that skimmed her large hips. The bodice of the dress was styled in a lighter color and texture than the skirt. Softly draped, elbow-length puffed sleeves widened her shoulders and balanced her wider hips. Her body looked balanced because skillful proportions were used to make her look sensational!

To demonstrate different proportions, imagine three women all the same height standing side by side. The first person has a large frame with bust and hip measurements balanced, yet she has a short shoulder-to-waist length and average leg length (crotch to feet). The second person may have a smaller frame with a longer shoulder-to-waist length and shorter legs. The third person may have a large bust and smaller hip width, be high waisted, and have longer legs. Another example is my daughter and me. We are the same height, yet when we sit beside each other, she looks taller than me because she has a longer torso. This indicates that we have a difference in body proportions, even though we are the same height. No matter what your body type, the aim is to balance the distance across the shoulders with the breadth of the hips/thighs by using proportional balance and scale. For example, when wearing a jacket, a person with wider hips than shoulders needs the jacket length to finish above or below the hip level. This will draw the eye away from focusing on the hips and thighs.

To get an accurate evaluation of your figure type, stand straight with arms by your side looking into a full-length mirror so you can see your full body length. Then determine which of the five body shapes describes you. Here is a description of each body shape with ideas of what to wear to complement your proportions:

Rectangle (same-size bust and hips and little waist definition)

What to wear to enhance proportions:

- Styles which create the illusion of having curves around the bust and hips and not the waistline.
- Sheath dresses are perfect for you!
- Fitted pencil or pegged skirt narrowing at the hem to create a curved shape over the hips.
- Tall rectangular people can wear wide-legged pants beautifully. Keep pants tapered for average-height or smaller women.
- Jackets that flare out at the hips give the waistline more definition.
- Skirts/dresses with a wider hemline create the illusion of a smaller waist.

Oval (fullness in tummy area)

What to wear to enhance proportions:

- Styles with detailing above the bust, such as the shoulder area, and below the hipline.
- Longer tops over pants with tapered legs.
- Tops with vertical or diagonal stripes.
- Square and V-shaped necklines.
- Pant styles that sit smoothly in the front with no fly-front zippers.
- Styles which draw the eye away from the waistline.

Hourglass (shoulders and hips the same width, with clearly defined waistline)

What to wear to enhance proportions:

- Styles to accentuate your waistline, whether you are petite or larger.
- Fitted styles following your body line.
- Gathered or pleated skirts.
- Belted waistline.

Triangle (shoulders narrower than hips)

What to wear to enhance proportions:

- Styles that draw attention to the upper body in bright colors.
- Darker colors for pants and skirts.
- Horizontal stripes on the upper body.
- Boatneck or round-scoop neckline to accentuate shoulders.
- Small shoulder pads in jackets to balance wider hips.
- A-line and full skirts that skim over the thighs/hips.
- Empire-waist dresses and flared, longer-length cardigan will glide over larger hips and improve proportion.
- Avoid pockets on the hips.

Inverted triangle (shoulders wider than hips)

What to wear to enhance proportions:

- Styles that draw attention to the lower body.
- Avoid too much detail on tops—wear simple tops.
- A-line skirts and pegged skirts to emphasize the hips.

Wardrobe Wisdom

- Avoid empire waistlines and strapless, off-the-shoulder, and halter tops.

Another helpful guide on how to dress for your body type is to use three-part proportions. To do this, divide the body into three equal parts and then create your "look." For example, a long, ankle-length skirt worn with a top finishing an inch or so below the waistline (or high hip) is balanced because the skirt covers two-thirds of the body and the top one-third. Ankle-length pants worn with a tucked-in top and a three-quarter-length cardigan is also balanced according to this concept. Following on from this, a short skirt worn with a hip-length jacket is balanced because two-thirds is the jacket length and one-third is the skirt. In these outfits, three-part proportions are used, which looks pleasing to the eyes. How about trying this with other garment combinations? It can make a dramatic difference in what suits your proportions.

By using proportion and balance, various components of an outfit and various fashion accessories can look good in relationship to one's size/body frame. A person can look bigger/smaller or shorter/taller by using proportion and balance. By using proportion, you can not only visually change the perception of someone's size but also their length. Jenna Coleman, who plays Victoria in the Masterpiece series, knows how much she needs an alterations specialist, because it can be difficult to find garments to fit her size. Coleman said, "Tailoring is key . . . I'm 5'2" and curvy, so I often try on dresses and think, 'This will never work.' But once something is fixed to your exact proportions, it's absolute magic."[15]

Proportion and Balance Style Advice

Having worked in the custom-made clothing industry for many years, it still amazes me how a particular silhouette (and style) can enhance a client's shape and take pounds off. The secret is to use diversionary tactics to direct attention away from your problem areas and emphasize your more attractive area(s). This can be done

15. Jenna Coleman, qtd. in Simon, "12 Things to Know," para. 2.

by using line, color, and styling. Line draws the eye in a certain direction, such as horizontal, vertical, or diagonal. Line can be used to balance proportion and figure problems. Let me explain. The cut and styling of a garment create lines. I coauthored a book which explains this concept well: "Structural design refers to all the seamlines that are stitched to hold the garment together."[16] For example, a horizontal line could be a waistline seam, pocket edge, belt, wide lapels, or stripes. A horizontal line has a widening, broadening effect. Further, adding a contrasting, colored belt to a garment can emphasize the horizontal line. Generally, horizontal lines are great for tall women because their height is shortened. Vertical lines, on the other hand, add length and height because the eye is drawn to look up and down. For this reason, vertical seam lines or stripes create a slimming effect. The use of vertical lines is also seen in a long cardigan or a scarf hanging lengthwise around the neck. Diagonal seam lines also create a slimming effect. An example of diagonal lines would be the shape of jacket lapels or stripes on an angle. A curvy figure looks better with the use of curvy design lines using seams, and a straight body type looks better with straight design lines in its seams. Also, the aim of using lines in design is to draw attention to your face.

When a tall person wears a sleeveless top and a short skirt (showing arms and legs), she will look even taller. Instead, wear a short-sleeve top or a long-sleeve top with short skirt or shorts. Tall people can break up their length with layers and colors. They can also wear wide or narrow horizontal stripes and wide belts to make them appear shorter. To make a shorter person look taller, wear vertical stripes. Additionally, altering the length of a skirt, dress, coat, or pants to give better proportions is one of the simplest alterations for an updated "look."

Let me illustrate how I use balance and proportion to my advantage. I'm 5'10" tall with a straight body shape and slim hips, and I am short waisted with little waistline definition. To create the illusion of better proportions—to disguise my short shoulder-to-waist length—I wear my jeans on the upper hipline with a

---

16. Cole and Czachor, *Professional Sewing Techniques*, 11.

belt—*never* on the waistline. The horizontal belt draws the eye across my body to give the illusion of wider hips. Then, a partially tucked-in T-shirt hanging over my jeans is intentional to create the illusion of having a longer torso. In contrast, a long-waisted person can shorten their torso by wearing a wide belt on the waist.

It can be hard for some people to discern what proportions suit their body type best. One way forward is to consult a personal image consultant or wardrobe stylist. They will explain why some styles do not suit you and then direct you to styles which do suit your body shape and proportions best. This was a wise undertaking that I invested in over twenty years ago. I still use this advice today. I will never forget the stylist saying to me, "Do not wear a V-neckline, because it will make you look like you have a giraffe neck." I have never worn a V-neckline since!

Which Are the Best Styles for You?

- A *well-fitted jacket* such as a blazer instantly adds a layer of polish to any outfit. A jacket is dressy enough to wear for professional occasions, relaxed enough to wear with your favorite jeans, and smart enough to be worn for an evening out. A hip-length jacket should cover the crotch if worn with pants. On a shorter person, a jacket that is too long will overwhelm the body and make a person look smaller. A double-breasted jacket adds width and bulk. If you want to appear thinner and taller, avoid big collars; if they are too big, they will make you appear bigger. Jackets with snugger sleeves are more slimming. If you have a large bust, wear three-quarter-length or long-sleeve lengths. If you have broad shoulders, narrow the shoulders by removing the shoulder pads.

- *Pants* automatically make a person appear taller. A beautifully tailored pantsuit in one color will slim the body. Cropped pants may look unflattering on people who do not have height. They shorten already-short proportions. Combining an oversized top and bottom will overwhelm your form.

Instead, pair one snug-fitting garment with one that has a more-relaxed fit. For example, pairing skinny pants with a loose-fitting top will create good proportion. This look suits most body types and looks stylish worn with flats, boots, or heels. Instead of wearing wide-leg pants, try cigarette-shaped pants/jeans tapered to the ankle to get a slim look. Shorten a long torso by wearing high-waisted skirts and pants.

- *Necklines*: let's face it—not all *neckline* shapes suit everyone.

  - A *low-cut scoop neckline* displays the collar bone and elongates the neck. Be aware that a low-cut neckline does not look good on a saggy, sun-damaged chest and neck. A person with a short neck looks best wearing a low-cut scoop neckline. It also flatters women with narrow shoulders because it makes the shoulders appear wider. For bustier women, wear a high-cut scoop neckline.
  - A *V-cut neckline* makes a short neck appear longer and gives the illusion of a longer, leaner silhouette.
  - A *wide-cut scoop* neckline enhances the bustline, and a boat neckline broadens the shoulders.
  - A *boat-cut*[17] or *square-cut* neckline is "just right" for a person with a long, elegant neck.
  - A *square* neckline or sweetheart neckline can be worn by most people.
  - A *strapless style* does not flatter everyone. It is most flattering on women with wider shoulders and a small-to-medium bustline.
  - A *turtleneck*, classy and warm for winter, is not the best style for a person with a short neck but is ideal for the person with a long neck.

---

17. A neckline shape which runs horizontal along the collar bone. It draws the eyes out to the shoulders.

Finally, if your body proportions are not ideal, they can be addressed. Everyone can dress in smart ways that flatter their body proportions.

Colors That Suit

When we are looking for a new article of clothing, color is the major deciding factor in most purchases. Often when we meet someone, color is the first thing that they notice about us. It was Laura Bush who said, "Nothing attracts attention like a red dress."[18] Red can be known as "sexual red," as it communicates love, passion, power, or sin. In Melbourne, black is the color of the day. In Britain, black is also popular. It is called "international black." Black can also communicate dignity, mourning, death, sophistication, etc. Wearing white can communicate virginity, purity, innocence, delicacy, etc. Indeed, our color choices tell the world a lot about our personality. I have a dear friend who is tender, gentle, and sweet in character. She wears soft pastel colors that suit her personality exactly. Another friend is bold and extroverted; she wears bright, vibrant, colorful clothing. My favorite colors are reds and coral. I am told this identifies me as an extrovert. How true!

The color wheel devised by Isaac Newton explains color relationships and helps our understanding of mixing colors and color schemes. The wheel begins with red, blue, and yellow, placed in equal distance from each other on the wheel. These are primary colors, and in fashion, they create a bold, vibrant statement. All other colors are mixed from these three major colors. When equal quantities of two primary colors are mixed, orange, green, and violet variants are created. These are called secondary colors. Subsequently, when a primary and secondary color are mixed, tertiary colors are created: variants of red, oranges, and yellows, which are warm colors; and greens, blues, and violets, which are cool colors. When white, black, or gray is added to a primary, secondary, or

---

18. Bhatt, "Lady in Red Quotes," para. 29.

tertiary color, muted colors evolve. Floral prints are often produced using this color effect.

We can all wear colors on the color wheel, but the color that suits me best may not suit you. Let's consider red by way of example. Audrey Hepburn said, "There is a shade of red for every woman."[19] The actress was onto something! The red that suits my complexion best is a secondary blue-red color. My sister's red is the primary color red, and my good friend Kristen wears a tertiary orangey red. It was a client, Robyn, who asked me, "Which buttons look best on my black coat, gold or silver?" I suggested gold, as it would look best with her complexion. She looked at me with a baffled look.

How, then, would Robyn have known what I was talking about? The key is whether your skin undertone is cool, warm, or neutral, no matter how light or dark your skin is. There are other factors as well, but this is the most important one. To begin understanding the skin undertone for you, look at the underside of your wrist. Examine it. If the veins appear bluer or deep purplish, your skin has a cool undertone. People with a cool undertone usually have a pinkish complexion. If your veins are greenish, you have a warmer skin undertone. You will have traces of peach or golden in your complexion. People with a neutral skin undertone will have an indeterminate vein color.[20] Another way to help to determine your skin tone is to observe how a silver watch or bracelet looks on your wrist and then how a gold watch or bracelet looks. Silver looks best on skin with a cool undertone, and gold complements skin with a warm undertone. Robyn obviously did not know this concept! This is where the seasonal color theory is a helpful guide to identify colors that suit your complexion. I emphasize that this is just a guide and not a rule!

The color theory divides colors into seasons—winter and summer (cooler) and autumn and spring (warmer). The colors relate to colors on the color wheel. One of these color palettes will suit your complexion best. Each color palette includes pastels

---

19. Bhatt, "Lady in Red Quotes," para. 36.
20. "Best Colors," para. 6.

Wardrobe Wisdom

and bright shades. A professional color analysis can determine this for you. It is economical and worth the investment because you receive a color palette to refer to. You can also go online to get a color analysis. The color palette you receive will save time and give you a sense of direction when shopping for clothes. This knowledge will help you be more thoughtful about your purchases. When you are aware of the colors that suit you best, you can quickly scan racks of clothing or accessories when shopping and spot the ones appropriate for you. This saves time!

A Brief Description of Each Color Palette:

Do note that people with a neutral skin undertone have the widest range of colors to choose from. They look great wearing colors such as mauve, mint, champagne, jade green, dusty pink, gray, and black, just to mention a few. Wearing bright primary colors will not enhance a neutral skin tone.[21]

WINTER

Think primary colors—clear, intense, vibrant colors such as black, navy, charcoal, pure white, true red, cobalt blue, hot pink, emerald green, and icy color tones.

SUMMER

Think muted (blue-based) colors tinted with white to soften the tone. These colors will look best on women who have a natural softness in their coloring—navy, off-white, powder blue, rose pink, raspberry, wine, watermelon, lavender, deep-sea green, and many other green/blue colors.

---

21. Gustashaw, "What Colors Look Best," para. 11.

Faith and Fashion

AUTUMN/FALL

Think in earth shades—rich golden brown; warm, deep olive; yellows of the sunset; dusty orange (terra cotta and pumpkin).

SPRING

Think colors with golden undertones that produce a warmed look. Neutrals are brown and nude tones, ivory, and camel rather than black—apricot and coral, turmeric, toffee, aspen gold, periwinkle blue, dusty blue, and aqua are a few other colors.

Your palette of colors will work well together in your clothing. You can wear them unwaveringly all year round. These colors will complement your complexion. Any dark circles will be less noticeable and your eyes will sparkle and give some life to your hair color. One way to know if a color suits you or not is to stand in a place with good light. Wrap a certain color of fabric around your neckline and upper-chest area. Close your eyes and then open them. Observe what you see. If the color suits you, it will stay in the background and your face will be noticed first. Additionally, wearing the "right" makeup colors will give you a final, polished look.

Some colors will not suit you. Wearing colors that do not suit your skin tone will drain the color from your face. Are you aware that black does not suit everyone? Black is the base color and default position for so many people because it is easy to wear, does not soil easily, and goes with everything. Black and white look great on my friend Julie, but they do not suit me. Instead, navy, burgundy, and taupe are the base colors that are best for me. Sometimes color coordination can be extreme! One day, I looked at my husband dressed ready to speak at an event, and even his burgundy Bible was color coordinated with his burgundy outfit. Accidents do happen!

How, then, does color affect your wardrobe? When you follow your color palette as a guide, you can be certain that your clothing and accessories will mix well. When you stray from your best colors, your wardrobe will not fluidly mix and match. The following story illustrates my point: One occasion when browsing the gift shop at the Milwaukee Art Museum, I found a table of reduced-price scarves. With only a glance, I plucked *one* out of a big pile that was in my color palette. I knew the scarf would coordinate with my existing wardrobe. I checked the fiber content, and I was delighted that the scarf was a wool/cotton mix. This was the perfect blend for warmth and comfort, and the material's texture was pleasing to the eye. So I purchased the scarf. When I tried on a variety of skirts, tops, and pants, I wrapped my new scarf around my neck. To my delight, I discovered it could be worn with at least six different outfits. Did I need another scarf? No! Was it worth buying? Absolutely!

Color Style Advice:

Did you know that certain colors can affect the perception of your shape and your weight? For example, light colors such as white and ivory enlarge, while darker colors such as navy and black are slimming. Perhaps that's why black is so popular! Then again, if you are heavier in the hips and thighs, wear dark colors to minimize this area. Monochromatic dressing, which is wearing clothing items in a variation of the same color, makes everybody appear taller and slimmer.[22] The trick with monochromatic dressing is to break it up with a pop of color or print in your shoes, bag, belt, or jewelry. Additionally, creating layers using texture and color in different tones and tints and varying hem lengths can create an interesting style.[23]

Color blocking is another way to flatter your shape, because it has body-slimming benefits.[24] Let's consider a person with large

---

22. Feldon, *Does This Make Me*, 33.

23. Tones are created by mixing a pure hue with a neutral gray. The value (intensity of color) can range from light to dark. A tint is when pure colors are mixed with white. The color remains the same, only lighter. These are pastel colors.

24. Color blocking is a styling feature that uses two or more blocks of contrasting colors strategically placed in an outfit to give the optical illusion of the

breasts or a large upper body. When wearing a top and skirt, choose a darker-colored top to minimize the upper body and a lighter or brighter color for the skirt or pants. For a person with larger hips, do the reverse—wear a darker hue to slim the hips and make your lower body appear smaller. Then pair with a lighter/brighter-colored top. Also, wearing a jacket in a brighter color—plain, striped, or printed—will draw attention to the upper body and balance wider hips and thighs. Sheath dresses with two vertical seamlines create panels (columns). Color blocking can be used to advantage on this style of dress. For example, for a person with a larger bust and curvy hips, the center panel should be in a lighter color and the two side panels in a darker color. This will minimize the hip width and give the illusion of less curviness. Do the opposite for someone with a small bust and hips.

Color can also be used to visually balance body proportions. Colors such as navy, charcoal, and black will minimize and are slimming. Lighter colors maximize and create a focal point. For a person with fuller hips and narrower shoulders, wear navy, black, or dark-gray skirts or pants. To create a pleasing visual balance, wear a white or light-colored top which has more volume to draw attention to your upper body. This will create the illusion of having balanced body proportions. An all-over print will camouflage body imperfections as well.

When I was a student studying fashion design, one fashion rule was "Never mix red and pink together." That rule flew out the window years ago! So be encouraged to express yourself by trying something new. Enjoy playing around with colors and find out what colors work for you. Try a fresh look; play with a mix of styles in colors, prints, and textures—some will work, and some may not. Finally, there are no absolutes! It was Coco Chanel who said, "The best color in the whole world is the one that looks good on you."[25] I will add to this: . . . and that brings you joy and makes you feel wonderful!

---

body looking slimmer.

25. Coco Chanel, qtd. in Samaha and Hyde, "Best Coco Chanel Quotes," para. 32.

Wardrobe Wisdom

Your Personal Style

There is no style formula. Dressing in a "chic" way does not entail rules.[26] Designer Oscar de la Renta is credited for saying, "Fashion is about dressing according to what's fashionable. Style is more about being yourself."[27] This includes giving yourself permission to dress in what you are attracted to and feel comfortable in—in colors that suit your complexion—rather than dressing in the latest, most up-to-date trends. Your personal style also includes personality and your preferences, interests, and values.

American model and actress Lauren Hutton is credited for saying the following quote that explains the difference between fashion and style: "Fashion is what you're offered four times a year by designers. And style is what you choose."[28] Still, it must be pointed out that finding your personal style can take years—even decades. I do not want to discourage you; rather, I hope to encourage you to give it time for your personal style to evolve. If you do not know what your personal style is today, do not worry, because with maturity and life experience, your style will develop. As we discover our personal style and pay attention to these things, we will feel more put together, perform better, and feel more confident.

Before we style ourselves, first we need to view ourselves as God sees us (unique, valuable, and unconditionally loved). God loves us just as we are, regardless of whether we dress stylishly or not; regardless of our body shape, our height, or the clothing size we wear. We cannot expect our clothes to give us worth. Feeling loved, accepted, and valued by God is what gives us ultimate worth, not what we wear and how we look. If we feel self-conscious in what we wear, think negativity about ourselves, and have low-self-esteem, it saps our energy and sucks the life out of us.

As a fashion designer, people think I have it all together as far as putting a stylish look together. Yet, I do have a wardrobe crisis

---

26. "Chic" (from French) refers to a woman who looks stylish.

27. Oscar de la Renta, qtd. in Harper's Bazaar Staff, "Greatest Fashion Quotes," para. 42.

28. Hutton, "Fashion Is What . . ."

now and then. I often ask my husband's opinion. Over the years, he has become my fashion consultant, and he is a theologian! We both chuckle about this. So, on occasion, I ask Graham if he likes a certain outfit I am wearing and if it looks flattering on me. This comes about when I explore a new design aesthetic. On one occasion, this was his wise response: "How you feel and how you look aren't necessarily the same. We can be too hard on ourselves." Even if we think we know our personal style and wear what looks contemporary and appropriate to our life stage and the occasion, at times we struggle with a wardrobe crisis. We can feel concerned about how others view us. Not everyone is going to like what you wear.

Your style tells a story. Italian designer Miuccia Prada said, "Clothes should always represent your vision of yourself... or what you want to present—even if it's only for one night."[29] The only way we can learn what is our personal style is by knowing who we are, by having curiosity about ourselves. Above all, it begins with an awareness of your body shape and experimenting with a variety of garments, accessories, and colors. Ultimately, it is about having fun with fashion. How would you describe your style? For some, it is adventurous; for others, it is elegance and simplicity, casual/cool, or quirky and whimsical. For some, they may not be sure as yet. For singer Rihanna, her style is daring, adventurous, and unique. Creating your personal style can be eclectic—a mishmash of clothing styles. Your style may be like Ingmari Lamy, a Swedish fashion model in the late 1960s who said she has a "potpourri approach to dressing." Her style is a mix of hand-me-downs, designer pieces, and flea-market finds. Her philosophy of fashion is "to love the poetry of the clothes I choose to wear."[30]

The most important part of discovering your personal style is to *be you*! We can wonder why certain styles do not work for us. Perhaps it is because you are wearing something that does not suit your shape or age group or that is inappropriate to wear on a certain occasion. Perhaps you feel pressured to look "perfect," to

---

29. Miuccia Prada, qtd. in Bowles, "Miuccia Prada," para. 7.
30. Ingmari Lamy, qtd. in Borrelli-Persson, "Model Ingmari Lamy, para. 3.

have a great body, and to always look glamorous. Do not use fashion to project a different persona. Do not copy another person's "look," as it may not reflect who you are. Iris Apfel, the flamboyant, ninety-plus fashionista, has a signature style that tells a story. She is credited for saying these wise words: "What's my style is not your style, and I don't see how you can define it. It's something that expresses who you are in your own way."[31] Be inspired by another person's style, but make it your own. It is about feeling comfortable in your own skin. It does not mean sacrificing style for comfort. In France, the phrase used is *bien dans sa peau* (well in one's skin), which often also refers to clothes and how you wear them, so it seems fitting. Victoria Beckham's style advice is "Trust your gut, not a stylist or a rule maker. There is nothing worse than seeing a woman out in clothes that she obviously thinks she should wear. Her discomfort is what you see first."[32] True style is not necessarily about wearing the latest trends.

Personal style is also about knowing how to compose an outfit. Good taste is seeing something that is in harmony and balance and is pleasing to the eye. It is a learning process to develop good taste and can take time. It is about having an awareness of what works for you without looking like a fashion victim. If you need specialized style help, a friend with good taste may be able to give wise advice. A consultation with a professional stylist can also be a wise investment. A stylist will give you practical expertise and explain which styles will suit your body shape and proportion best.

Style is not only expressed in fashion but is also articulated in the way you live, the décor of your home, the way your garden is planned, and how you set the table for a birthday celebration, Thanksgiving, or Christmas. Your style is also influenced by your cultural values, upbringing, hobbies, and environment. For example, a woman deeply rooted in Texas, the "Lone Star State," may wear denim and cowgirl boots as part of her style. Part of my Brethren Church upbringing was to dress up for church. It is designer Kate Spade who is credited for saying, "Playing dress-up

---

31. Iris Apfel, qtd. in Juma, "Fashion Quotes," para. 18.
32. Victoria Beckham, qtd. in Rubenstein, "Victoria Beckham," para. 5.

begins at age five and never truly ends."[33] To this day, I still dress up for church, as it is rooted deeply within me from when I was a little girl.

Iris Apfel tells a story by her signature style. She wears oversized, iconic eyewear and over-the-top jewelry as she walks the streets of New York. She was once told by Frieda Loehmann, "Iris you're not pretty, you'll never be pretty, but you have style."[34] Iris does not have any fashion insecurities. She feels complete freedom to dress how she sees fit! Some people, like Iris, wear flamboyant, brightly colored, exaggerated clothes; and some wear conventional or edgy clothes. Additionally, others feel more comfortable wearing easy, simple clothing with minimal color. Then again, some people dress carelessly, telling the world that they do not care, cannot be bothered, feel frumpy, or perhaps even feel lazy.

One day, I asked my husband, "What story am I telling about my life by what I wear?"

He answered, "Style matters; function matters; fit matters; context matters; and [my] husband's opinion matters!"

Personal Style Advice

Wise women are always learning and listening, asking questions, and continually seeking fresh insights regarding their personal style. To know your style, begin by asking yourself these practical questions: What shape of tops and pants/skirts do you like—fitted, relaxed fit, or a loosely fitted, oversized silhouette? What colors do you like—dark or light, bright or muted? Do you like prints, plain fabrics, or textured fabrics, etc.? What types of fabrics do you enjoy wearing? Next, gather several pieces of clothing and try them on. This can be in a store dressing room or at home. Observe how they look and feel on your body. Also, do some homework. Go window shopping and look at fashion magazines, online stores, or Pinterest. Create a portfolio of what you like and what you think suits

---

33. Kate Spade, qtd. in Juma, "Fashion Quotes," para. 98.
34. Freedman, "IRIS," para. 8.

Wardrobe Wisdom

your figure. Keep it updated as your style evolves. Still, you may find certain styles you love and decide to stick with them.

Creating layers using textures and colors in different tones and varying hem lengths can create an interesting style. When rock star Fergie was asked about her personal style, she said "her wardrobe... is like her musical taste: unpredictable: hip-hop, club, synthesized, with a little rap thrown in, with a recent injection of gritty rock 'n' roll. Each genre of music has made a mark on her style."[35] It can take time to find your personal style. Do not give up, because style evolves over time and will be fluid. Tennis champion Venus Williams said this about Rihanna's style: "I love that she is herself with no apologies. Her sense of style and self is unique. I love how she transforms herself with each album, each campaign. Always evolving."[36]

If you do not wear a certain item the way other people do, then do not get distracted by what other people think. They do not live your life. Try not to compare yourself with others or be influenced by their taste. As a personal example of taste, I found a piece of wall art online that I loved and considered purchasing because I liked the unusual shape, texture, and colors. I showed several friends and family—some loved it, and others did not like it at all. I could have been persuaded to let it go. Did I purchase it? Yes, because it was so "me." Carolina Herrera, the flawlessly clothed designer, insists that when she has a consultation for a custom-made bridal gown, the bride must come alone. This way, her friends and family cannot influence or sway her too much. Herrera said, "It's one of the most important days in her life. She should be able to wear what she wants."[37]

Accessories are a practical way to create a personal style. Shoes and handbags can add a pop of color and zing to an outfit. When it comes to accessories, scale is important. People with height can accessorize with large or oversized handbags and chunky jewelry. For a petite person, accessorize with modest-sized bags to give

---

35. Zee and Edt, ELLEments of Personal Style, 46.
36. Venus Williams, qtd. in Long, "Rihanna," para. 34.
37. Carolina Herrera, qtd. in Martin, "Carolina Herrera," para. 13.

a better sense of proportion. Iris Apfel is credited for saying this about accessories: "These are things I love, things I've worn. I get more compliments on accessories than anything else."[38] If you're wearing basics, such as jeans and a white shirt, add some pizzazz to your look by accessorizing. Try chunky jewelry, dainty pieces, a belt, a scarf, or a hat. Not everything has to cost a huge amount to create your personal style! I own a "low-cost," ten-dollar, chunky locket chain purchased many years ago. I am often asked if it is vintage. It is not. This necklace is one of my favorite pieces which I can wear with just about everything.

Michael Kors said it succinctly: "Seventy percent of the clothes you own should be meat and potatoes. Thirty percent should be icing and fluff—that's color, pattern, shine, and accessories."[39] Over coffee one day, my friend told me this story about her mother. She always viewed her mother as having style. She presumed that her mother owned lots of clothes, because she always looked so beautifully put together in so many different outfits. When clearing her mother's wardrobe upon her death, she was surprised to find minimal clothing. She realized it was the scarves she wore that created so many different looks.

We All Change

Your style today is most probably not going to be the same as it was five, ten, or twenty years ago. For example, I wore hot pants in the seventies. Would I wear them as a mature woman? No! Most of us are not the same person as we were when we were younger (nor do we have the same figure). You probably have different opinions about style as you mature and grow.

Having nailed a look, you will have the confidence to say, "This is who I am; this is what I like to wear; this suits me; and I feel comfortable." Of course, having a wardrobe full of beautiful clothes is not necessarily going to change you and make you feel

---

38. Iris Apfel, "These Are Things . . ."
39. Cline, *Conscious Closet*, 101.

Wardrobe Wisdom

confident. Ultimately, knowing who you are in God's sight means you can walk out the door feeling confident and knowing you are loved and precious no matter how you dress. Now that is freedom!

Lastly, ask yourself, Does it really matter if you make a fashion mistake?

Wardrobe Organization Advice

Creating a functional, organizational system that works for you will streamline your choices when deciding what to wear each day. It also makes mixing and matching your clothing seamless. When your wardrobe is organized, you can immediately see what your dressing choices are. If room permits, space your clothing so every garment can be seen. Some people sort their clothes by colors and/or garment types. Personally, I like to organize my wardrobe in groupings of clothing: skirts together; shirts, tops, and cardigans together; dresses together; and pants together. I do this separately for summer and winter clothes.

Lastly, some final wise words from New York author Elizabeth L. Cline: "When every garment has a purpose and every color and cut goes with something else, your wardrobe can carry you through life and style, no matter the occasion."[40] We are made in the image of God no matter how we are dressed. Christ died for us no matter how we are dressed. Believing these truths can utterly transform your life.

Wise the Bible's Way: A Reflection by Graham

We live in a "knowledge society."[41] Those with knowledge succeed, so we are told. That is why many see a college education as crucial to success. However, from the Bible's perspective, there is a difference between knowledge and wisdom. Put simply, wisdom is

---

40. Cline, *Conscious Closet*, 94.
41. Castelfranchi, "Six Critical Remarks," 1–3.

knowing what to do with knowledge. Said another way, it is knowledge on steroids.

The book of Proverbs is filled with wise sayings and illustrations of what biblical wisdom is. For example, in Prov 6:6–11, there is a contrast between the foolish person and the wise person, a common contrast in the Bible. Winter is coming, and so what does the foolish person do? The lazy person puts their feet up: "A little sleep, a little slumber, a little folding of the hands to rest" (Prov 6:10). Then a reversal of fortunes comes: "And poverty will come upon you like a robber and want like an armed man" (Prov 6:11). By way of contrast, consider the ant (Prov 6:6). Proverbs describes ants as "small, but they are exceedingly wise" (Prov 30:24). The wise person is like an ant. Ants are industrious. The ant stores up food for the coming winter and so survives (Prov 6:7). The point being made is that a wise person knows how to observe the way things work and their relevance to this matter or that. In the case of the ant, the wise person learns from observing nature. Regarding fashion, the wise person observes what their body type is and dresses accordingly.

There is another aspect to biblical wisdom worth noting: the wise person is also a teachable one. Openness to learning is vital to living wisely. In Proverbs, children are to listen to parental instruction, whether from the father (Prov 1:8) or the mother (Prov 31:1). No person of any position in society is beyond the need to be a learner, even kings, like Lemuel (Prov 31:1–9). This book is filled with things to know about fashion. Readers need to be open to learning them. It is a safe bet that the very fact that you are reading this book shows that openness.

Simply knowing things, however, is not enough. More is needed to be wise. For example, I know how to put a screw in the wall. You drill a hole and put it in. You do not hammer it in. However, you also need to put in a plug before you put in the screw. Application can be done badly—just try putting in the screw without the plug. This book is full of suggestions as to how knowledge can be applied in ways that fit the reality of who you are and your stage of life.

Wardrobe Wisdom

The most important aspect of biblical wisdom has to do with attitude. Being knowledgeable is not enough. Even knowing how to apply knowledge the right way is not enough. Being clever is not enough. The wise person adopts a particular stance toward God: "The fear [reverence] of the Lord is the beginning of knowledge" (Prov 1:7). That reverence may show itself in you praying before shopping for clothes so that you be a good steward in doing so. We live life *coram Deo* ("before God"), as the Reformers of the sixteenth century taught (e.g., Luther). That is wisdom the Bible's way.

Chapter 5

The Thoughtful Fashion Consumer

> Don't be into trends. Don't make fashion own you, but you decide what you are, what you want to express by the way you dress and the way to live.
>
> GIANNI VERSACE

> Buy Less, Choose well, Make it Last.
>
> VIVIENNE WESTWOOD

WHAT, then, as a thoughtful follower of Christ, should our attitude be as consumers in general and of clothing in particular? What can be concerning is the time it takes to maintain our possessions and whether they dominate our lives and make us feel discontented, resulting in wanting more possessions. In and of themselves, possessions aren't bad. The challenge is how to be a thoughtful consumer when new things come on the market which can leave us wanting more and more.

The Thoughtful Fashion Consumer

A Minimalist Approach to Fashion

Joshua Becker—a writer, blogger, and speaker on Christianity—is inspiring others to own less and apply minimalist principles to their possessions, and this includes clothing. He says that when we feel insignificant, it can tempt us to overconsumption. He suggests that "the message of minimalism can counteract that feeling of emptiness by focusing more on the things we truly hold important: family, joy, fulfillment, love." He then poses the question: "Was Jesus a minimalist?"[1] Consider Jesus' words in Matt 6:19–21: "Do not store up for yourselves treasures on earth, where moths and vermin destroy, and where thieves break in and steal. But store up for yourselves treasures in heaven, where moths and vermin do not destroy, and where thieves do not destroy, and where thieves do break in and steal. For where your treasure is, there your heart will be also."

Snezhina Piskova is just one of many people "obsessed with buying clothes."[2] Working as a copywriter in the fashion industry, she was surrounded by people who had a fashion-obsessed way of thinking. This impacted her! She said, "I would buy 10 pairs of very cheap jeans just for the sake of having more diversity in my wardrobe for a low price, even though I ended up wearing only two or three of them."[3] To keep the manufacturing costs low, garments are often produced in low-wage countries such as China or Vietnam. Much of this apparel is of low quality, cheap and mass-produced. Cheap prices lure us to buy more clothing that we may not need. How many cheap clothes have you purchased, worn once or twice, and then thrown out? I'm sure many of us have fallen into this trap of buying this type of clothing, including me!

Why is it that we over-purchase and under-use clothes? This question is explored by clinical psychologist Mike Kyrios, who works in one of Australia's universities researching mental health disorders. He believes that "a lot of things we purchase fulfill

---

1. Erickson, "Joshua Becker," paras. 8, 10.
2. Ro, "Can Fashion," para. 2.
3. Ro, "Can Fashion," para. 2.

some kind of function in ourselves—particularly fashion items... People who have lower self-esteem or worry about their status are especially likely to use overspending as a route to feel like they 'belong.'" Additionally, he believes that people are trained to find impulse buying pleasurable and addictive. He suggests that a better approach for people with compulsive buying habits is to find other, less wasteful ways of achieving a sense of reward. One way he suggests is to ration the time we spend shopping for clothes online.[4]

Interestingly, in 1930, the average American woman owned nine outfits. A survey done in 2020 by ClosetMaid, a business installing home shelving for closets, revealed that the average American woman owned 103 items.[5] Do we really need this much clothing? With an increase of clothing items are we any happier and do we have a more functional wardrobe? No matter how many clothes we own, it begs this question: "Is your closet working for you?" It was interesting to read in this article that "21 per cent [of our clothes] to be 'unwearable,' 33 per cent too tight and 24 per cent too loose," and 10 percent of us are depressed every time we open our closets."[6] I enjoy watching the TV show *House Hunters*. My observation of people searching for a house is that they want a large kitchen, at least two or three bathrooms, and a really large walk-in closet! I'm not against large houses and large closets. We just need to be aware of the clothes we gather and the space we need to house them.

You may be asking: How, then, can I be a minimalist with my clothing needs and own a closet of clothes that works for me? If we follow the French way of dressing (explained in Appendix 2) and prioritize purchasing minimal clothing made from quality fabrics and constructed with quality workmanship, it will help to address these concerns.

4. Mike Kyrios, qtd. in Ro, "Can Fashion," paras. 41–44, esp. 41.
5. "Struggle Is Real," paras. 3, 5.
6. ClosetMaid, "How Many Clothes."

What about Fads and Trends?

A fashion trend is a new design that has been accepted, has taken hold, and lasts. Once a trend takes off, we do not know how long it will last. Some trend cycles turn over quickly. One season something is "in," and then the next season, it's "out." For example, skirt lengths go up and down and silhouettes change. In the 1970s, if you didn't wear a miniskirt, you were not on trend. Today, every length of skirt is acceptable. I think we're more relaxed about trends today. A fad is a trend that is short-lived and does not last. Most trends run about every two decades and are often a reintroduction of past fashion. For example, Bridget Bardot, the French actress, singer, and fashion model, wore off-the-shoulder tops in the 1960s. This trend, which leaves the shoulder bare, has resurfaced again.

Trends keep people in business. Glossy fashion magazines set the trend agenda for shoppers. Many shoppers also take their trend cues from social media. For example, after Taylor Swift went on TikTok wearing a pretty, floral, lemon-colored, strappy dress retailing at $218, it instantly sold out in all sizes![7] Hollywood celebrities such as Sarah Jessica Parker and Katie Holmes are also trendsetting style influencers. Models such as Jean Shrimpton, Cindy Crawford, and Kate Moss have been style and trend influencers too. Fashion muses such as Audrey Hepburn, Princess Diana, and Michelle Obama (just to name a few) are others. Giants in fashion, such as Christian Dior, Coco Chanel, and Vivienne Westwood, have also been influential trendsetters. Rihanna, the celebrity superstar singer, is also a major style influencer and owns her own fashion line. Whether she is walking the streets of Paris or New York, on the red carpet, or at fashion week, she captures attention whether she is wearing outrageous jeans, an evening gown, a pantsuit, or a short dress. She is iconic and never ceases to surprise us by her bold glam looks.[8] Rihanna is also the queen of Instagram and uses it to promote her style.[9]

7. Allaire, "Taylor Swift."
8. Hoby, "Rihanna," paras. 1–10.
9. Bowen, "Queen of Instagram."

What's happening globally can also influence emerging trends and shape the direction of fashion. For example, when the United States went to war with Iraq in 2003 and overthrew the government of Saddam Hussein, military-inspired fashion was popularized. At the time, I designed and stitched a coat inspired by a US Civil War uniform. I am still wearing it today! A sociocultural force can also create a design shift. Coco Chanel, the greatest style icon of the twentieth century, insisted that a design shift was necessary in the Victorian era. She believed women needed to be liberated so they would feel freedom and comfort in their clothes. So she pushed to eliminate the need to wear a corset.[10] Thank you, Coco!

Even a pandemic can influence the direction of fashion. While quarantining at home, many of us wore comfortable loungewear/leisure wear all day while working remotely and attending Zoom meetings. Fashion magazines tell us how the demand for loungewear increased during the COVID-19 pandemic. Emily Farra, senior fashion news writer for *Vogue*, says, "There's a reason we've never connected loungewear with fashion or considered it part of our actual style." Yet, no fashion authority could ever have predicted that the only apparel category to grow during the COVID-19 pandemic would be loungewear![11]

Fashion forecasters are market-research specialists who analyze and provide reports about trends that expect to materialize a year or two in the future. What the fashion forecaster is looking for is a fresh, new, original style to trickle down into mainstream fashion. Fashion forecaster Linda DeFranco recalls that her boss, after a fashion-forecasting trip, showed photographs of teenagers in Stockholm "wearing their jeans rolled up a few inches to make them tighter around the legs." From this point, DeFranco and her colleagues "predicted a coming trend"—skinny jeans—and "by 2006, skinny jeans were all the rage."[12] By 2010, the style was es-

---

10. "How Coco Chanel Freed Women," para. 6.
11. Farra, "Loungewear," paras. 1–2, esp. 2.
12. Zimmerman, "Roaming the World," paras. 1–2.

tablished. The title of a *Guardian* article in January 2013 confirms this fact: "Skinny Jeans: The Fashion Trend That Refuses to Die."[13]

As consumers of clothing, we also need to be aware of the current trend of "fast fashion" (like fast food). Fast fashion is immediate—the timeline is compressed—so clothing seen on the runway or worn by a celeb goes into stores immediately. Fast-fashion clothing can be cheap knockoff copies of designer high-end fashion brands sold at low prices using cheap labor. Meghan Markle's exquisite wedding gown designed by Clare Waight Keller took 3,900 hours to design and create according to some accounts.[14] This is approximately five and a half months. Just six days after the royal wedding, a bridal company had produced a cheaper knockoff version.[15] Fast-fashion clothing can be alluring. They appear to be a great bargain because they are inexpensive, so we buy them. The more consumers buy cheap clothing, the more demand there is, and so more cheap clothing is churned out and we buy more, and so on . . . Fast fashion is worrisome because it encourages a throwaway mentality. Fast fashion also encourages overbuying. Perhaps fast fashion contributes to our overstocked wardrobe and eventually adds to landfills.

There are some trends that will work for you and some that won't. Charles Manning, senior style editor for *Cosmopolitan* magazine, says, "Fashion is about following trends, but style is about finding a look that works for you and sticking with it. You'll never be satisfied chasing trends. Find what works for you and go with it."[16] Awareness of your personal style will help you sift through trends. If you want to dress in the latest trends, only wear it if it suits your figure type and your age group. Recently, I was reading in *Vogue* how one trend for fall that year was the reintroduction of pants from the 80s. The style was high waisted—belted—with a cinched waist, front pleats, and loose, wide legs. Is this pant style going to suit everyone? *No*! Even though I have the height to wear

13. Cocozza, "Skinny Jeans."
14. Goldstone, "Royal's Wedding Dress," paras. 1–3.
15. Puente, "Royal Wedding Gown Knockoffs," para. 3.
16. Manning, "14 Important Lessons," para. 8.

them, this trend is not going to be the best style for my figure/body type or my age.

Indeed, trends can be great for adding some flair, and new experimental ideas can individualize your look. Even so, if you are drawn to a certain seasonal trend, it is wise to limit the amount you buy.

Finally, "nothing you wear is more important than your smile!"[17]

Fabric Savvy

Some time ago, I was in a restaurant with Graham enjoying a southern BBQ meal. The restaurant was crowded, and we soon knew why. It was trivia night. The host was striding up and down the aisle between tables trying to get dining enthusiasts ready to answer questions about movies, famous people, and objects in well-known museums. As he passed by me, he said, "You are a material girl." *Yes*, I am a material girl! How did he know this, I wondered?

Without getting too complicated, let's define "textiles," "material," "cloth," and "fabric." "Fabric" is the word used for textiles. Fabric is the cloth or material produced by weaving or knitting cotton, wool, or silk threads or yarns into fabric. "Material" refers to the ingredients the fabric is made from. For example, you may ask about the jeans I am wearing today: "What type of material are they made from?" My answer would be cotton. In this text, "fabric" is used when referring to making clothes.

A thoughtful consumer pays attention to the various characteristics of the material a garment is made of and buys the best quality they can afford. Wisdom begins by learning some fabric savvy. Let me ask—how many of us know the exact kind of fabric they are wearing today? Is it woven or knit? There are two categories of fabric: woven and knit.

---

17. This quote is attributed to Connie Stevens (Stevens, "Nothing You Wear . . .".

Woven fabric weaves threads on a loom in a vertical direction and a horizontal direction, and they interlace at right angles with each other. Woven fabric does not stretch. When a small percentage of Lycra or spandex is added to a woven fabric, it will have a minimal stretch for comfort.

Knits are formed by rows of yarn loops continuously interlocking together. Knits are a favorite among many people because they stretch, hold their shape, and offer unrestricted comfort. Designers Donna Karan and Calvin Klein (among others) manufacture a significant number of knits (in jersey for example) in cotton; cozy, warm wool; and cashmere. Knits with Lycra or spandex will have extra stretch, fit-flexibility, recovery (keep better shape), comfort, and ease. This category of knit is perfect for performance garments, as they provide for maximum range of motion.

Fiber Is Good for You

Fibers are the basic element of fabric. They are long, thin filaments of thread that can be knitted or woven into fabric. Many people have no idea what types of fiber they are wearing. This is unfortunate, because the type of fiber that a garment is made from indicates its quality and characteristics. It also affects the fit and flow as well as appearance, cost, performance, how the garment will wear, how it launders, and how comfortable it feels. The fiber also indicates whether you'll feel cool or warm. It also influences how to care for the garment. For example, if the garment is made from silk fibers, dry cleaning will be recommended. A garment made from cotton fibers can be machine washed. Knowing these details will give you wisdom in not only choosing the style, color, and fit but also in the maintenance required.

Let's look at the three major fiber categories: natural, synthetic, and regenerated. Part of fabric savvy is to be able to identify what type of material you are wearing. Knit and woven fabrics can be made from any of the following materials.

Natural fibers derive from plants and animals. Cotton, linen, silk, wool, cashmere, mohair, and alpaca are all-natural fibers that we mainly use for fashion garments. (Other natural fibers are hemp, ramie, and jute.) Natural fibers have the benefit of being renewable resources. They keep farming communities in business and are important to our economy. Many natural fibers treated with fertilizers, chemicals, and pesticides are not easily biodegradable (i.e., capable of decomposing). The more fertilizers, pesticides, and chemicals used in the textile industry, the longer a fabric takes to decompose.[18] Certified-organic cotton, linen, and bamboo are eco-friendly fabrics that are biodegradable and will not clog up landfills. If wool is treated *without* chemicals, it is also biodegradable.

- *Cotton* is the most common fiber and is much loved. Clothing articles made from cotton are a wardrobe staple. Cotton garments have excellent qualities, such as the following: breathability, absorbency, and moisture-wicking properties which allow for ventilation to keep you cool on hot, humid days.

- *Wool* insulates you and keeps you warm. It was interesting to hear on the news on a super-freezing Chicago day this recommendation: "Do not wear cotton next to your skin, as it will not keep you warm; wear wool."

- *Linen* is produced from flax plants. Linen was a familiar fiber worn in biblical times. For example, Aaron the high priest wore four linen garments: "He is to put on the sacred linen tunic, with linen undergarments, next to his body; he is to tie the linen sash around him and put on the linen turban" (Lev 16:4). Linen has great qualities. It's strong, long wearing, very absorbent and fade resistant, lint free, and crisp to the touch. Linen is perfect to wear on hot days when you want to feel cool and breezy. However, linen easily wrinkles.

- *Silk* is a wonderful, breathable fabric that can be worn year-round in almost any climate. It's delicate, lustrous, light-to-medium weight, and comfortable to wear. The care

---

18. Feldon, *Does This Make Me*, 120.

instructions on the label on silk clothing will mostly recommend that the garment be dry-cleaned.

Synthetic fibers are man-made and are almost always created from chemical compounds. Synthetics include polyester, nylon, acrylic, spandex/Lycra, and microfiber. As stated previously, spandex/Lycra adds stretchability to fabrics. Synthetics cost less to buy and are easy to care for. Sadly, cheap, fast-fashion, knockoff styles are mostly made from polyester. Journalist and fashionista Elizabeth Cline, in her book *The Conscious Closet*, points this out about polyester:

> Polyester is by far the world's most dominant fiber, accounting for more than half of all global fiber, fiber output and more than 80 percent of all synthetics. Without polyester, there could be no fast fashion—it is the cheap, easy to produce material that an industry built on low prices and speed depends on. Polyester is plastic. It is made by refining crude oil or natural gas, breaking it into chemicals, and creating polymer that is extruded and spun into fibers.[19]

Synthetic fibers are *not* breathable like natural ones. When clothing made from polyester is worn in summer, you can feel hot, clammy, and sweaty. Because of this, polyester requires more laundering in comparison to woolen garments, which require minimal washing. Regardless, there are many synthetics that do have moisture-wicking properties which pull dampness away from the skin. Also, synthetics do not add warmth in winter. However, they are great for travel because they are wrinkle resistant.

Regenerated fibers are manufactured from natural materials such as wood pulp from eucalyptus, beech, or bamboo trees which are chemically processed into fibers.[20] Rayon material is made from regenerated fibers and is extremely popular for clothing because it is soft to the hand and drapey and breathes well. Unfortunately, it

---

19. Cline, *Conscious Closet*, 162.
20. Cline, *Conscious Closet*, 170.

does have the potential to shrink when laundered. Viscose, modal, bamboo, and lyocell are also regenerated fibers.

Blended fibers combine the best qualities of two or more fibers to enhance the quality of a fabric. A typical blend is cotton/polyester or linen/polyester. Both cotton and linen crush. When a percentage of polyester is added to cotton and linen, the fabric will crush less and will be easier to launder. Another blend is wool/spandex. Wool adds warmth, and spandex adds stretch and comfort. A blend of cotton/rayon will feel soft next to the skin. In some cases, a fiber blend may be a better choice than choosing a garment made from natural fiber. Elizabeth Cline offers this good advice: "In extreme cold weather environments, some percentage of cotton and wool mixed with highly durable nylon will ensure that the fabric doesn't freeze, so it might last longer than those natural fibers alone."[21]

Cline also offers wise advice on choosing fabrics that are sustainable: "When in doubt, choose natural fibers or viscose rayon for everyday wear and intimates, as they will give you the sense of feeling comfortable. If you're buying a garment made from a blend of fibers, make sure that at least 50 percent of the fiber content is a natural fiber or viscose rayon."[22] Recently, I purchased a cotton sweater, and to my delight, it was manufactured from recycled cotton. The cotton is repurposed from scraps of yarn and fabric, garments, towels, and other household items which are converted into cotton fibers. This approach to sustainability in the textile industry is laudable, because the discarded cotton fibers are reused rather than thrown away.

Fabrics also come in different weights (light, medium, and heavy). It is advisable to check the "hand" of the fabric of any garment you intend to buy. Technically speaking, the hand of the fabric is what you feel when you touch it, and doing this tells you if a fabric is light, medium, or heavyweight and whether that piece of clothing will feel dense, light, or airy to wear. By handling the fabric, you also get a sense if it is smooth, rough, stiff, silky, soft, or

---

21. Cline, *Conscious Closet*, 86.
22. Cline, *Conscious Closet*, 60.

textured. This lets you know how a garment is going to feel when it's worn against the skin. Some fabrics can feel scratchy, (e.g., lace and some wool fabrics). You need to feel no irritation from any fabric you are wearing. Recently, I was shopping with my daughter. After finding a garment she was attracted to, next she touched the fabric to feel the softness/harshness. Then she looked at the garment tag and took note of the fiber content. It was after this that she considered whether to buy the garment or not. I realized I had taught her well!

Fabric also has a drape characteristic to it. The drape of a fabric refers to how the fabric flows and moves on your body. Softer, lightweight fabrics such as satin silk; a sheer, lightweight georgette or crepe; and many knit fabrics are soft and drapey. Heavy, stiffer fabrics such as denim and textured tweed do not drape. These fabrics are better for fitted, tailored garments. Bulky fabrics such as quilted cloth (with two layers of fabric); chunky knits; fur; and fuzzy, textured fabrics make you look bigger, as do shiny fabrics, because they have a reflective surface.

High-quality fabric feels good next to your skin and produces superior seams and a superior fit. Brands that produce this quality will cost more and are a bigger investment. I have a merino-wool jersey dress that I made and wore to a wedding in 2006. The stylishness of the design and stitching is still just as good today as it was back then, partly due to the high-quality fabric. Garments made from low-quality, cheap fabrics will only last one or two seasons before they begin to look worn.

How to Purchase Wisely

There is no universal rule regarding which clothing to buy. Your must-have clothes will be different than your best friend's must-have clothes. Everyone's needs will be different according to their lifestyle, favorite colors, comfort level, and body type.

It is not the cost of the garment that makes it valuable. But if a garment, accessory, pair of shoes, or belt is expensive, the item may still be worth the cost if it mixes well with your existing wardrobe and gives more variety to your outfits. To evaluate its worth, look at the cost per wear (CPW). To calculate this, take the total cost of the item and then divide this by the number of times you can wear that item to find the CPW.[23] Using this calculation will let you know if an item is a good buy or not. According to the CPW calculation, is a cheap, fast-fashion dress costing forty dollars and worn once at a party a good buy? No! The dress is a bad buy and not cheap, because the CPW is forty dollars![24] Now let's look at a quality, $600 leather handbag which can be worn every day. The CPW is 1.65 over a year. This is value!

Do some research before shopping—look in brick-and-mortar stores and online stores, in magazines, or on Pinterest. Keep a file of the styles you think will suit you. Be intentional about which garments you choose to buy. Thoughtlessly buying whatever takes your fancy is not wisdom. If you buy online, it may involve buying several styles in a few sizes and returning the ones that do not fit you or suit your wardrobe plan. If you are purchasing from a brick-and-mortar store, take at least two sizes into the dressing room. Try both on and choose the one with the best fit. Look for quality-investment pieces that last.[25] As you browse in stores, ask the salesperson to hold the items you're interested in so you can think about them before purchasing. If you shop online, look first, put the item in the cart, and then leave it a day or two to think about whether it is the "right" piece of clothing for you or not. Many times, you will forget about the item, which means you probably do not need it or can't afford it. If it stays in your mind, then consider buying it. Do not purchase any item unless it can be returned. This advice also goes for shoes, bags, and accessories, etc.

So that you do not over-purchase, take the following advice:

---

23. Cline, *Conscious Closet*, 153. I have taken the concept of CPW from Cline but calculate it differently from her.

24. Cline, *Conscious Closet*, 154.

25. More on this in Appendix 2.

The Thoughtful Fashion Consumer

- Have a plan: list what you need to buy. Do a thorough assessment of what your clothing needs are right now to fill in the gaps.
- Have a budget. Listen to your wallet! Decide which items most of your money will be spent on.
- Allow plenty of time to shop. Put a day aside. Do not rush your decisions. Ask a friend to come alongside you. This person needs to understand you and be able to offer an honest opinion.
- Buy from stores with a good return policy.
- Hit the dressing room prepared: wear the correct undergarments. Take the shoes that you plan to wear with the outfit, because the higher the heel, the shorter the length will look. Take any other clothing that you want to mix with any new purchases.
- Only buy things you love rather than things that you think you should wear—incorporate your personality into your clothing choices.
- Avoid impulse purchases and shopping because you are bored.
- Buy quality, not quantity—put more money into timeless *basics* you know will mix and match and color coordinate with your existing clothes.
- Spend less on trendy items.
- Check the fibers and ask whether they are sustainable and long-lasting.
- When you have an outfit on, determine the following: Does the silhouette suit your body type and size? Do you feel comfortable sitting and moving in the garment? Do the colors suit your complexion and brighten your face?
- Pay attention to the fit, look in the mirror, and check every angle—front, side, and rear. Determine if the garment is too tight/big around the bust, waist, or hip area. Look at the

overall garment length and sleeve length and ask yourself if it is too long/short? No panty lines should be noticeable in any outfit, so check this as well.

- Check if the garment is well-made. To do this, look at the overall stitching to determine if the seams are stitched securely and lay flat. Pull the zipper up and down to see that it works smoothly. Also check that the hem is stitched securely. If the garment has buttons, check that each one is stitched firmly. If your garment has a checked pattern or stripes, you may want to note if the checks/stripes match at the seams.
- When you add a new item, delete an existing one to keep your wardrobe in check.
- Take good care of your clothes.
- Wear what you buy with confidence—keep fashion fun!

Good Stewardship

God cares about what we do with what he gives us. All that we have belongs to the Lord, including our clothing and the accessories we buy. As Christians, this should influence what we spend on our clothing and how much clothing we should own, including the time we put into looking for clothes and how much time it takes to care for them.

The psalmist tells us in Ps 24:1, "The earth is the Lord's, and everything in it, the world, and those who live in it." Hugh Welchel, executive director of the Institute for Faith, Work & Economics, comments on this verse: "We are called as God's stewards to manage that which belongs to God."[26] The money we have belongs to God. For this reason, we need to be responsible stewards of our resources, money, and time. Another aspect of our stewardship is to be concerned about how we treat the land we live in.

Part of good stewardship can be simplifying our lives and having a minimalist approach to the things we own, including

---

26. Whelchel, "Four Principles," para. 12.

The Thoughtful Fashion Consumer

clothes. I need to be reminded of how God wants me to be a good steward of what he has given me. So I ask myself this question: How many clothes should I have, and how much should I spend on materials? This is when I need a good biblical perspective on stewardship and how I should spend my time and money when it comes to clothing and accessories.

God requires us to keep our lives clear from loving money. Hebrews 13:5 says, "Keep your lives free from the love of money and be content with what you have." I do not always find this advice easy to follow myself. Benjamin Franklin is credited for saying, "Money has never made man happy, nor will it, there is nothing in its nature to produce happiness. The more of it one has the more one wants."[27] I wonder if Benjamin Franklin read this verse from Eccl 5:10: "Whoever loves money never has enough; whoever loves wealth is never satisfied with their income. This too is meaningless."

Materialism can be a temptation as well as a trap. Imagine that your family is buying a new home. You demand a large closet for all your clothes and excess garage space to house all your surplus belongings. What we want and our excessive desires can hurt family relationships and bring financial pressure. We cannot take our belongings (stuff) with us when we die. It is alarming to read about the trend in the US that "82% of homes have two-car garages or larger, but only 15% use them to park the car inside."[28] Similarly, in the UK, "53 percent of households have access to a garage, only 24 percent use them for parking cars."[29] With this phenomenon, the garage is not used for its purpose of housing the car but for storing excess stuff. Think about all the storage units being built to house the extra "stuff" we accumulate. Perhaps it's time to purge your closets of stuff!

Rather than being materialistic, we are to be content with what we have yet shrewd with our resources; we must know how to use our money wisely. We are encouraged to be like the woman in

27. Franklin, "Money Has Never . . ."
28. Lynnette, "Garages Aren't for Cars," para. 8.
29. Lynnette, "Garages Aren't for Cars," para. 7.

Prov 31, who worked hard with her hands, provided for her family and her servants, was thoughtful about her business endeavors, and saw that her work was profitable. She knew what to invest in and made wise and honorable choices. Then she opens her arms to the poor and needy in generosity. Above all, she is "clothed with strength and dignity" (Prov 31:25). Like this woman, part of our faithful stewardship is to give generously in service to others. I constantly need to ask the Lord to give me contentment in what I have, because new products advertised on social media and elsewhere can make me feel dissatisfied with what I already have. We can feel pressure to own a huge, gorgeous home and to be styled in luxury goods, designer clothes, pearls, rubies, diamonds, and the list goes on. We all live with desires that are not fulfilled, because we can't always have what we want.

Wealth is not negative or evil. It can be positive. Abraham knew financial blessing (Gen 13:1–2). Psalm 31:19 says, "How abundant are the good things that you have stored up for those who fear you, that you bestow in the sight of all, on those who take refuge in you." Money is harmful if we love *it* more than God. Luke 16:13 is clear: "No one can serve two masters . . . you cannot serve both God and money." Revering God is the secret. This is to live in awe of a holy God and to live with a grateful heart for all that God has given us (e.g., creation, home, work, and clothes on our back).

When it comes to our clothing, awareness of what to invest in is important. How we spend our money will differ depending on what we like to wear, what we value, how each new item fits with our existing wardrobe, and—of course—what we can afford. When we consider our overall income and how much money we must spend, include a clothing budget, because it will provide a limit on the number of clothes we purchase. How we use our clothing budget will differ. For example, someone may purchase *one* quality-leather handbag worth $700 or more. For me, this would be an expensive handbag. Yet, for another person, it may not be expensive but rather worth it because that *one* handbag will last for many years, will be used every day, and goes with everything else in her wardrobe.

The Thoughtful Fashion Consumer

I loved to visit Macy's department store on State Street when I visited downtown Chicago. Not only do they have a gorgeous Tiffany dome ceiling in the atrium, but they also have great clothes, accessories, makeup, and other luxury goods to purchase. On one shopping trip, I was looking for taupe-color boots to fit with my wardrobe. I found a pair that I really, really wanted. I felt conflicted as I wrestled with the "right" decision, because I *so* desired them! As I grappled with my longing to own the boots, I soon realized I already had a similar pair that went with my color palette. It was then that I knew I didn't need them.

I constantly need to ask myself if I need something even though I desire it. My budget does not allow me to buy everything I desire. Overspending beyond our means is not wise or honoring to God. Knowing what to invest in is important. To illustrate this point, imagine you see a pair of purple high-heeled shoes that you love. They look gorgeous and make your legs look oh so slim and elegant. Without too much thought, you purchase them because you look so fabulous wearing them! When you get home, you realize you have nothing to wear them with; neither do they suit your lifestyle or your color palette. Now you need to buy a new dress, necklace, earrings, and bag to match your new purple shoes. These extra purchases add up, and suddenly, you have blown your budget! Were the purple shoes a wise investment and a good stewardship choice?

Getting your clothes altered is another good stewardship decision. An alteration is less expensive than buying a new garment. A "fresh look" can be created by the expertise of an alteration specialist by updating the fit. A garment can also be repaired, such as replacing a zipper, taking up a hem, or restoring/replacing a lining. I own many coats because I lived in Chicago, and the winters there were brutally cold. Recently, I tried on one of them, which I had made many years ago from luxurious alpaca fabric. It now felt drab and dowdy. Since the fabric was of high quality, it was worth restyling to give it a new appearance. Even the duchess of Cambridge, Kate Middleton, knows the value of a "recycle-and-reuse moment."[30] Having worn a printed, off-the-shoulder, couture black dress by designer Alexander McQueen to a celebrity event in London in 2017, she looked stylish once again wearing the same dress to a gala event in 2019 with a new upper bodice restyled with cap sleeves. I did smile when I read, "The strategy is clearly royal approved."[31] Next time you are invited to an elegant event, perhaps consider wearing one of your existing dresses you have hardly ever worn and that is still hanging in the closet and having it restyled.

We can spend way too much money on our clothes and accessories or too little money buying cheap, low-quality clothes. So aim for quality in cut, design, and workmanship. One way to save money is to *not* shop thoughtlessly!

Finally, whatever we own should glorify God. Overspending is not wise or honoring to God. The challenge is how to be a thoughtful consumer.

What We Love Matters: A Reflection by Graham

Thinking about money or the lack of it can totally consume a person. Perhaps this is why "there are over 2,300 verses in the Bible that deal with money and possessions."[32] This multitude of biblical references suggests that money and possessions can really affect our relationship with God and with others. Psalm 62:10 is a good example of a biblical warning about money: "If riches increase, do not set your heart on them." How many of us have fought with our spouse or children over the cost of something? The fact is that loving money too much indicates a lot about our character and the measure of our commitment to Christ. Positively speaking, we need to spend our money wisely, whether we're using it to pay off a house or car loan or whether we're buying clothing. The Bible is clear: wealth is not an evil. Money can be used for good or evil.

---

30. Allaire, "Kate Middleton," para. 1.
31. Allaire, "Kate Middleton," paras. 2–3, esp. 3.
32. "Living Your Faith," para. 2.

The love of money is the problem, as Paul taught Timothy (1 Tim 6:10).

In the famous Sermon on the Mount, Jesus taught: "Don't store up treasures on earth! Moths and rust can destroy them, and thieves can break in and steal them. Instead, store up your treasures in heaven, where moths and rust cannot destroy them, and thieves cannot break in and steal them. Your heart will always be where your treasure is" (Matt 6:19–21). The reference to moths only makes sense if fabric is in Jesus' mind. I had a van once that I really loved. It was brand new when I bought it. I loved showing it off to friends. I went through a phase of Toyota evangelism. That is, until I hit a semi head-on on a highway and my van was written off. Thankfully, I was able to walk away from the wreck, as was Jules and our children. Amazingly, no one was hurt. The police officer was mystified as to why none of us had been killed. My heart had been in the wrong place. My van had value, but not that much value.

We can love beautiful clothes and the money we use to pay for them, but beautiful clothes cannot love us.

Chapter 6

The Ultimate Wardrobe Change

By Graham Cole

THE good news of Jesus Christ is about transformation. The New Testament is dramatic. The change is passing from darkness into light (1 Pet 2:9), from death to life (John 5:24). It is finding yourself in the divine law court and God, the Judge, declares you acquitted (Rom 8:33). It is being a slave in the marketplace, but God pays the price to redeem you and set you free (1 Cor 7:23). It is being an orphan, but then God adopts you as his son or daughter (Gal 4:4–7). This is good news indeed. And notably, it is about a change of clothing: the ultimate wardrobe change. In the Bible, a change in clothing can symbolize a change of fortunes. Think of the famous story of the prodigal son that Jesus told (Luke 15:11–32). The son comes back after having wandered far from home and his father. The father not only greets him with a loving embrace but also has him clothed in the finest of robes. The son knows he has been welcomed, much to his older brother's disgust.

Biblical scholar Brian Rosner captures the Bible's teaching about clothes in a striking way:

> The Bible is about clothes, used not only to denote community identity, signal social status, and enact legal agreements, but also and more significantly to illustrate God's redemptive activity. From the first act of mercy

extended to fallen humanity, the covering of Adam and Eve with clothes, to the end of the age, when the community of the redeemed will be clothed with an imperishable, immortal, heavenly dwelling, the exchange and provision of garments portray God's gracious and redemptive provision.[1]

Let's explore further how references to clothing can give us insight into what it means to come into a relationship with Christ and to follow him.

Coming to Christ

When you think about it, trust binds persons together. A marriage without trust is doomed—so, too, a friendship and a business partnership. The New Testament talks a lot about faith, meaning trust. The apostle Paul states in Gal 3:26: "So in Christ Jesus [i.e., in relationship to him] you are all children of God through faith [trust]." What he writes next is striking (v. 27): "For all of you who were baptized into Christ have clothed yourselves with Christ." The clothing metaphor signals a great change.

The early church saw the significance in the metaphor and turned it into a practice. Philip Kosloski describes what happened in Rome around 215 AD according to a document attributed to Hippolytus, an early church leader:

> The *Apostolic Tradition* explains how those to be baptized must "remove their clothing," and go into the water "naked." Scholars debate the extent to which baptisms were "naked" and whether or not it simply meant the outer garments, or all clothes. In either case it spiritually represented a particular "death" to the old self and a firm departure from sin. It was a physical reminder that they were to be born a new person in baptism and had to cast off their old ways, discarding their old clothes in order to put on the new life in Christ.

---

1. Rosner, "Biblical Theology," 10.

Faith and Fashion

> Immediately after baptism the newly baptized would put on a white garment, which represented the cleansing of their sins and the purity of their soul, born anew in the font of baptism.[2]

The laying aside of the old garments and the putting on of a new, white garment—symbolizing purity—must have made for a dramatic sight.

One of the towering figures in Christian history is Augustine (354–430 AD). His conversion story is famous. He was sitting in a garden reading. He heard a child's voice say, "Take up and read! Take up and read!" So he did. He opened the text at Rom 13:13–14, and it addressed his life directly, as he had lived a promiscuous one by his own account. In his autobiography, he relates:

> So quickly I returned to the place where Alypius [a friend and another seeker, like Augustine] was sitting; for there had I put down the volume of the apostles, when I rose thence. I grasped, opened, and in silence read that paragraph on which my eyes first fell—Not in rioting and drunkenness, not in chambering and wantonness, not in strife and envying; but put on the Lord Jesus Christ, and make not provision for the flesh, to fulfil the lusts thereof. No further would I read, nor did I need; for instantly, as the sentence ended—by a light, as it were, of security infused into my heart—all the gloom of doubt vanished away.[3]

He put his trust in Christ and put on Christ. Paul's clothing metaphor was entirely apt for his personal history and situation.

But what does it mean to be clothed with Christ? John Calvin of the sixteenth century has wise words to offer as an answer: "But herein is the wondrous method of justification, that, clothed with the righteousness of Christ, they dread not the judgment of which they are worthy, and while they justly condemn themselves, are yet deemed righteous out of themselves."[4] Two metaphors are at work

---

2. Kosloski, "How Was Baptism Practiced," paras. 12–13.

3. Augustine, *Confessions*, bk. 8, ch. 29.

4. Calvin, *Institutes*, bk. 3, ch. 11, p. 616.

here. Justification conjures up images of the law court. The divine Judge looks at us. What will the verdict be? Justified and therefore set free, or condemned and set for judgment? The apostle Paul pictures the Christian clothed in the righteousness (rightness) of another (see 1 Cor 1:30, Gal 3:27). The divine Judge, as it were, sees Christ in all his rightness, not us in all our lack of rightness, because we are clothed in him.

The same great wardrobe change is available to all who today relocate their trust from themselves to Jesus Christ for their eternal welfare.

Following Christ

Coming to Christ, or becoming a Christian, is not the end of the story. We are called to follow Christ. This is the life of discipleship, and it, too, can be described in clothing terms.

The apostle Paul used the clothing metaphor to explain how Christians are to live. He instructs the Ephesians: "You were taught, with regard to your former way of life, to put off your old self, which is being corrupted by its deceitful desires; to be made new in the attitude of your minds; and to put on the new self, created to be like God in true righteousness and holiness" (Eph 4:22–24). Certain vices are to be intentionally stopped. Certain virtues are to be embraced. He has the same message for Christians at Colossae: "Do not lie to each other, since you have taken off your old self with its practices and have put on the new self, which is being renewed in knowledge in the image of its Creator" (Col 3:9–10). What are those practices? They include the following: "Sexual immorality, impurity, lust, evil desires and greed, which is idolatry" (Col 3:5). Positively, he argues: "Therefore, as God's chosen people, holy and dearly loved, clothe yourselves with compassion, kindness, humility, gentleness and patience" (Col 3:12).

A new identity means a new way to live.

Conclusion

What makes up the fabric of our lives? We cannot fool God by our external, glam appearance. God sees our heart. We may feel bitter, angry, and unloving inside but look fabulous on the outside. We need the ultimate wardrobe change, a change of heart. That ultimate wardrobe change happens to a person who comes to Christ and puts their trust in him. That's why the New Testament describes such people as "believers." Thus begins a way of life in which the new replaces the old. There are things to put off (vices) and things to put on (virtues).

Appendix 1
What Does a Fashion Designer Do?

People are often intrigued about my job as a fashion designer. They ask, "What does a fashion designer do?" Let me give you some insight into my profession. I work in a creative industrial space, and through the process of developing ideas, I create clothing. Overall, a designer works with their hands to create beauty. I work with a wide range of materials, such as a variety of fabrics, laces, jewels, skins, embellishments, and much more. In my case, I do not own my own business. My focus has been working for smaller companies to design clothing for women of all ages. These days, designers need knowledge of computer-aided design programs. However, I mainly use a pencil and sketch pad for my design work. My friends will tell you that I will sketch designs that come into my mind on napkins when I am meeting a friend for coffee and do not have a pencil and sketch pad on me.

My work also includes creating garment patterns and the use of large cutting tables, industrial forms (three-dimensional models of a torso—and some with legs—used for fitting each new design), all sorts of scissors, rulers, and sewing machines. My most prized tool is a tape measure! Many designers build their own brands. In my case, this has not been possible because of our focus on ministry. Some may be part designer and part businessperson, seamstress, salesperson, and/or production manager, depending on the demands of the company. Building a brand involves a lot of hard work. Irish designer Simone Rocha commented, "This decade has

Appendix 1

been how long I have been working on my collections ... It's been blood, sweat, tears, and beauty."[1]

Designers may rarely get to design what they like. Their job is to be focused on the customer, a company's vision, and brand identity. They must be flexible and adapt to an ever-changing world. Designers must keep their eyes open to what is happening in contemporary cultural and social contexts—celebrities, trends, new inventions, and products on the rise—because it can influence the direction of fashion. Fashion can also be shaped by a certain celebrity look, or fashion trends from past eras can be reclaimed and reemerge on the runway and on the street. War can influence fashion trends as well. The lack of accessibility to fabric during World War 2 resulted in clothing becoming more utilitarian. After the war, designs exploded to celebrate a sense of freedom, with the use of excessive amounts of fabric. Styles became soft, feminine, and romantic instead of merely utilitarian.

Artists, whether they are fashion designers, photographers, painters, or songwriters, need inspiration to keep their work fresh and their ideas original. The designer begins the same way a painter begins—with a blank canvas on which to paint an artistic composition. The design-development process starts with research, which is a journey to explore ideas and gain inspiration. These ideas are then developed all the way to the unique, finished garment(s). A garment is an artistic composition using the elements of design, such as line, texture, proportion, and color. Designers need to be gifted with drawing ability to illustrate and communicate designs. However, they do not sketch cute little dresses all day or design what they like. The designs also need to attract consumers. For a design to be successful, it *must* sell. Being a designer is not all glamor!

While on a tour of the Red Rocks of Sedona, Arizona, I was told by the guide that prickly pear cactus inspired Walt Disney to create the round ears of Mickey Mouse. Fashion designer Enoch Ho, a Hong Kong native, combines his faith with his creative work. He said, "If you walk a life of faith, there are constantly ideas,

1. Yotka, "Decade in Fashion," para. 10.

What Does a Fashion Designer Do?

topics, and stories that you come across that are an immensely deep well of inspiration."[2]

The successful designer must know their consumer. The garments should meet customers' needs, ages, and lifestyles and be affordable. Nevertheless, much of the clothing we see on runways and in fashion magazines is not wearable. Part of the designer's decision-making process is to ask the following questions of their garment: Is it wearable? Is it flattering? Do you get the best out of this dress? For a designer to know the customer, some questions need to be asked, such as the following: Who will wear the garment? What is her style? Where does she live? At what stage in life is she? How does she want to feel while wearing these garments? What story is she telling others when she puts the garment on? New York designer Christian Cowan says, "When I go through my designs, I think, does this capture people? Will they click on it if they see it online? Will a celebrity see it and feel like they must wear it? Will a woman walk into a store and feel confident and amazing in it?"[3] This may make you smile. I recall hearing a story about the designer Michael Kors and how his collection must be appropriate for his clients to wear while driving their convertibles to the clubs in Malibu! Even the rich and famous need to be catered to.

Designers need to have knowledge of fibers, fabrics, textures, weaves, and their distinctiveness. Fashion is visual, so selecting the "right" type of fabric for a certain design is fundamental to the success of each piece of clothing. This involves awareness of how a certain fabric behaves, attentiveness to how it feels, and observation of how it drapes on the form. For example, wool and cashmere insulate and provide warmth. Yet, wool can feel scratchy next to the skin. Linen feels crisp to the hand, but it is ideal to wear on hot days because it keeps you feeling fresh and cool. A wet suit, made from layers of synthetic rubber neoprene, insulates the body while in chilly water. Garments for skiing need moisture-wicking properties to keep you dry. Wearing leather protects a motorcyclist from injury. When swimming competitively, the characteristics of

2. Cheng-Tozun, "Enoch Ho," para. 2.
3. Farra, "Vogue Fashion Fund Finalists," para. 15.

Appendix 1

the swimsuit fabric—such as elasticity for ease of movement and quick drying—are especially important. Athletic apparel needs to be made from high-performance fabric that is durable and able to withstand stress and strain.

Designers need expertise in pattern-drafting techniques for garment making. Shaping the pattern is part of the creative process. How the patterns are made relates to the body shape. To do this, attention to each detail is necessary. For example, the neckline shape, position of each seamline, garment length, and button placement is proportionally planned on pattern templates. Coco Chanel, the French fashion designer, was so right when she said, "Fashion is architecture: it is a matter of proportion."[4] Patterns may be drafted by the designer, assistant designer, or a patternmaker. Designers also need knowledge of garment construction. They may not personally sew the garment, but they need sufficient knowledge of sewing techniques because they may need to instruct a machinist on how to stitch a garment with precision. During the creative process, sample garments are tested on "fit models" to achieve perfect sizing before they go into production. All aspects of the entire creative process of fabric research, pattern, fit, stitching, trims, and other details should be integrated. Each cannot succeed without the others.

The most important principle in the creative process is unity of design. Unity of design is the coherent mix of material, color, pattern, texture, and textile. For the designer, unity is the goal in any good design and must hold the viewer's interest. A design with complete unity has nothing overdone and nothing forgotten. The best test for a completely united design is the sense that not one tiny detail—not one line, shape, or trim—could be added or altered without spoiling the overall effect. Ultimately, you want a consumer to gravitate toward a particular design. Then, you want to hear the customer say, "I feel amazing in this!" Sometimes, designs are failures. Through failure, new and creative ideas are born. Finding out what works and what does not work is an essential part of being creative.

4. Jones, "History of Art and Fashion," para. 12.

What Does a Fashion Designer Do?

Designers create seasonal, ready-to-wear collections for the mass market or custom-made garments for individual clients. Custom-made garments are made to fit a client's body measurements, and this process is much more involved than buying a garment off the rack. The number of units in a collection depends on the size of the company. A collection of women's wear needs to be forward-thinking with an interesting balance of styles to appeal to a broad spectrum of women. For example, a line of casual wear could include skirts, pants, jackets, coats, and tops. Other collections may focus on one style category, such as swimwear, coats, bridal clothes, or evening wear. Another collection may have several groupings of women's wear, with different designers designing for each group; they may even be produced under different labels. For example, Liz Claiborne and Jones New York have six to eight such groups in each collection. A collection may also follow a theme and/or color story. Fundamentally, the collection needs to be cohesive. Every season, innovative design evolves to produce a collection that is creative, unique, and even avant-garde.

Clothing brands cannot reflect the taste of every woman. Each company has their own sizing and fit for their target consumer, and for this reason, a brand may exclude you. For example, a mature woman will not find clothes to suit her style, taste, and size at some stores because her age-group is not represented by their brand. It is worth finding a few go-to clothing brands that reflect who you are—your age, size, shape, and style. This can save shopping time. For example, some brands suit a curvy shape best, and other brands suit a straight body shape. I have found my go-to jeans brand which suits my straight body type and long legs. I am 5'10". The brand is not cheap, but it is worth the price because of the fit and styling.

Appendix 2
How to Build a Wardrobe the French Way

A woman has two problems:
1. Nothing to wear
2. No room for all the clothes[1]

One shouldn't spend all one's time dressing. All one needs are two or three suits, as long as they and everything to go with them are perfect.[2]

COCO CHANEL

How many of you have said, "I have a closet full of clothes and nothing to wear?" Perhaps it is because your closet is bulging with too many cheap clothes you have bought online, on sale, or on a whim. I was not surprised, then, to read this: one survey revealed that in the UK, almost one-half of the clothes in the typical woman's wardrobe have never been worn because they no longer fit or are no longer in style.[3] This is alarming!

1. "Nothing to wear."
2. Coco Chanel, qtd. in Cherylyoung, "Coco Chanel," para. 24.
3. Ro, "Can Fashion," para. 35.

How to Build a Wardrobe the French Way

Owning too many clothes can be confusing, because you cannot decide what to wear each day. It can bring about decision fatigue, especially for busy people. The same goes for owning too many shoes and bags. Having too many clothes squeezed into your wardrobe creates a dysfunctional wardrobe. Would you like to have a streamlined wardrobe and to know that every piece of clothing looks great on you and fits you well, with every piece working well in style and coloring? This is called stress-free dressing! Stress-free dressing means you can get dressed in five minutes knowing your outfit is coordinated and fits you beautifully and perhaps attracts a compliment.

Would you like to choose well and make your garments last? Women in Paris have a vastly different philosophy, and so they shop in a distinctive way. They have a less-is-more approach to fashion. This approach means having fewer garments, but better-quality ones that are built to last. The Parisian way of dressing is one way to be a minimalist and a good steward of our God-given resources, and a way to be more thoughtful about the clothing we purchase. We can learn from their wisdom, because it prevents excess purchasing. Since clothing is cheaper to purchase in America compared to European prices, we often over-purchase without any thought of what the quality of the garment is or how the new purchase will work with other clothing articles in our wardrobes.

French Fashion Secrets

The French woman is intentional with her buying choices. The plan is simple. She buys fewer items of clothing that are of good quality, last a long time, and are ageless. She chooses quality over quantity. She sees her clothing as an asset. She has minimal pieces in her wardrobe that work effortlessly together, and she wears them often. These are versatile separates. With minimal pieces, she can create multiple looks at any age. In the helpful book *Fashion Speak: Interviews with the World's Leading Designers*, David Meagher quotes designer Helmut Lang, who said, "Quality doesn't go out of style every six months."⁴ To dress like a French woman, you make careful decisions about your clothing choices. You choose them purposefully so that all items mix and match.

The French woman's buying method speaks fashion wisdom for all women—whether you are a stay-at-home mom, a retired businessperson, a CEO, or any other; whether you have a single or dual household income; whether you work from home or outside the home to earn a wage to support your family. By following this method, you will reduce the amount of clothes you own, spend less time getting dressed, and have more time to enjoy life. The French woman's fashion secrets are as follows.

First, she purchases *basic, timeless* pieces that become *staples* and the backbone of her wardrobe. "Basics" are foundational core pieces that give you a blank canvas. They are simple and elegant in style and cut. These are versatile garments that become the base of her outfits—garments such as pants, skirts, shirts, jackets, blazers, and/or a coat in neutral colors. Neutral colors are navy, burgundy, brown, taupe, beige/cream, black, white, and gray—not hot pink or lime green! Neutral colors work well as basics because they are timeless, will mix easily, and do not compete. These garments usually cost more due to the use of more expensive fabric, superior cut, and excellent stitching. The cut and shape of basics are always current, as they are classic in style and elegance. They can be worn for years and years. The French woman works all her outfits around her basic items. Designer Coco Chanel knew the secret. She said, "To my mind simplicity is the keynote of all true elegance."⁵

Sasha Skoda, head of The RealReal, which sells luxury consignment clothing, said in a 2020 *Vogue* article, "For the past year, it's been all about maximalism, but when COVID-19 hit we saw it take a backseat to stealth luxury . . . Shoppers are trading bold, logomania pieces for more timeless classics. Those may feel more appropriate for the current climate, and they're also smart investments."⁶ Skoda would endorse the fact that basic investment

4. Helmust Lang, qtd. in Meagher, *Fashion Speak*, 234.
5. Coco Chanel, qtd. in Feldon, *Does This Make Me*, 112.
6. Farra, "What's Selling," para. 5.

pieces are timeless classics which transcend the decade and trends, plus they have no expiration date.

If you feel like your basics are—yes—basic, then add some imagination and excitement with your "mixers."

A French woman then purchases "mixers." Mixers are less expensive accent pieces. They can be a top, cardigan, scarf, belt, or piece of fashionable jewelry. Mixers seasonally modernize a French woman's wardrobe and create a "new" up-to-the-minute fashion statement. Mixers can be fun—even exaggerated—and over-the-top pieces in avant-garde fabric prints, colorful patterns, different textures, and sparkles. Mixers multiply the combinations of possible outfits when paired with preexisting core pieces. A French woman does not spend too much on mixers unless it is an outstanding belt or piece of jewelry, or an outstanding pair of shoes that transforms the look of an outfit.

What Does Quality Look Like?

What are some characteristics of excellent-quality clothing, you may ask? For example, high-quality denim feels heavier and stiffer to the hand. Lightweight, low-quality denim suggests a lesser thread count with less durability. Clothing made with organic fabrics, especially ones that are fair-trade certified, will be crafted into sustainable, quality clothes. To test if the fabric is high quality, hold it up to the light with your hand behind the fabric (except if it is sheer). If you cannot see the outline of your hand, it implies that the garment is made from quality fabric. Excellent quality means superior durability, because each seam is stitched with more frequent stitches. If seams have been stitched with loose, longer stitches that are further apart, this is not quality stitching. To test if you have good-quality seam stitching, do this: hold the fabric on each side of the seam and pull outward. If you can see through the stitches, it is not quality stitching. Quality stitching always produces a better-fitting garment. High-quality garments have well-stitched buttons, pockets, and linings. They often include a spare button and thread so you can repair them if needed. This kind of quality *may* cost more, but owning less will hopefully balance the budget.

A quality garment is built to last. Model Victoria Lee, when asked what the oldest garment was in her wardrobe, said, "My Nan's going away coat from her wedding." This valuable woolen coat was still in excellent condition due to the quality fabric.[7] It is not necessarily only luxury couture that is high quality. Affordable, less pricey clothing can also be built to last.

Style Advice for Decluttering

If you struggle to choose what to wear each day, perhaps you own too many clothes and it is time to declutter. Basically, we only wear 20 percent of the clothes in our wardrobes, and these clothes are often the same ones we wear over and over.

What would your life look like if you followed what actress Drew Barrymore did? She loved to shop for clothes but did not shop with wisdom. She found her closet getting larger and larger but could not easily see what she had. To address her struggle with an overabundant closet, she put her closet on a diet and resisted the temptation to over-purchase. She explains how she did this by embracing a new relationship with clothes: "For starters, I'm almost 40, and the 20s clothes don't make sense anymore. And, after two babies, the 30s clothes don't fit anymore. I am at a clothing crossroads, and it's a painful one at times."[8]

To counter these feelings, Drew put herself on a "closet diet," limiting her wardrobe and only buying items thoughtfully. She says, "Months later, my closet is sane and I am happy. I don't have a battle every time I get dressed. I say to myself, 'You know what works, so just work it, and be good to yourself.'"[9]

You may also learn from this young mother from Dallas, Texas. She likened her disorganized wardrobe to the menu at the

7. Victoria Lee, qtd. in Gordon, "Fashion Mistake," para. 2.
8. Barrymore, "Closet on a Diet," para. 1.
9. Barrymore, "Closet on a Diet," para. 10.

How to Build a Wardrobe the French Way

Cheesecake Factory restaurant. Those of you who have eaten there are aware of the vast food options. Choosing what to eat can feel overwhelming with *so* many good menu options. To her, making style choices felt overwhelming like that. She went on to say that having a wardrobe with fewer pieces was like dining at an upscale, fine-dining restaurant with fewer dishes on the menu to choose from. By owning fewer but more versatile pieces, it is easier to put an outfit together.[10]

Maybe it is time to make some changes and purge and declutter! This means eliminating clothes that do not fit, out-of-date clothes, life-stage clothes no longer suitable, clothes in colors that do not coordinate, clothes that are unflattering for your shape, or items rarely worn. For some, it may feel daunting and overwhelming because it means a fundamental change. Perhaps you are a hoarder or have an emotional attachment to your clothes. Or you may have gained weight and your clothes no longer fit. This can feel disheartening. You may find it hard because some clothes have had special relevance or prompt a memory of someone who is no longer with you (such as a mother or grandma). It may even evoke a happy memory of when you wore that particular garment.

Decluttering is an intentional exercise. It is worth putting time into this project because your wardrobe will ultimately be more functional and fashionable when you own fewer garments. So why not ask an honest friend to help you? The opinion of a good friend who knows your style will be invaluable. Plan well ahead and put a day aside to do this. Make it a fun activity. Perhaps start with a glass of wine and music! Another way to approach this is to consult a professional stylist who will do a clothing inventory and guide you in which clothes to get rid of and which to keep from your existing wardrobe. Next, they will point you to some additional clothing that will work with your existing wardrobe.

---

10. Whitney, "What Your Bag."

APPENDIX 2

Declutter—Three Steps:

1. Empty your wardrobe and place everything on the bed.
2. Try on all your clothes. Examine each piece. As you do, ask a few questions: Have I worn this garment in the past year? How does it make me feel? Do I feel at ease wearing it, or am I always fussing with it? Does it make me look fabulous? Do I love it? Be ruthless and honest with yourself.
3. Make different piles of clothing:

    - Keepers: clothes that you love and feel confident wearing, suit your lifestyle, fit well, and are in colors that suit you. Group into classifications of pants, skirts, tops, etc.
    - Get rid of: shabby, torn, stained, worn-out, or pilled clothes.
    - Donate: clothes in colors that do not suit you, feel uncomfortable, no longer fit or are outdated, are no longer needed, or do not suit your lifestyle. Make sure these are still good quality clothes and not too worn and yellowed.
    - Repairs: clothes that need altering or need small repairs (replacing a missing button, patching a small hole, or shortening a hem).

Keep a few comfortable clothes for wearing around the house or for working in the garden. I call them "home favorites." If wardrobe room permits, you may want to keep some exceptional items you do not presently wear but may wear again down the road. (Be selective, and be careful not to keep too many of these types of garments.)

Decluttering can also be done for shoes. Sort through them and divide them into types: casual, dressy, sandals, boots, etc. Then do the same for handbags. Only keep the ones that are indispensable. The result of decluttering is that you can see every piece of clothing, because you will have more space in your wardrobe and more peace of mind, and maybe you will find it freeing. Can you imagine how easy it will be to get dressed in the morning when you have fewer garments and an organized, decluttered wardrobe system? It will take less time to choose a well-put-together outfit, leaving you more time for other more important tasks, such as caring for family, exercising, reading, or doing creative projects.

When discussing this with a friend recently after decluttering her excess clothes, these were her comments. She found a minimal wardrobe more manageable, she no longer felt burdened getting dressed in the morning, and she felt stress free when shopping, with a firmer sense of which clothing suited her body shape and proportions best. She also found that having less clothes to choose from calmed her spirit and helped her feel settled before getting on with her day. You may also find you will reinvent yourself.

Many women ask me how to build a coordinated mix-and-match wardrobe of basics and mixers. After you have decluttered, I suggest following the French woman's style secrets by building a cohesive wardrobe of basics and mixers.

Let's get started . . .

Basics and Mixers—Three Steps:

1. From the keepers clothing pile, divide them into *basics* and *mixers*. Getting the basics right is the starting point to building a well-coordinated wardrobe.

2. Try on your basics and mixers to see how many different looks you can create that mix in style and color coordination. Place these back in your wardrobe.

3. Take time to think about the key investment pieces you need to purchase which are needful and necessary to complete your wardrobe.

With your freshly decluttered wardrobe, I advise this—when dressing in the morning, choose a basic garment first, then choose which mixer you will wear with your basics.

New items can be purchased over time. Get to know brands that suit your body shape and style. If you find a brand of T-shirt,

Appendix 2

jeans, or pants that suit your budget and size and flatter your shape, then make it your go-to brand. It may save time and money to invest in two or three of the one item in assorted colors. Items such as scarves and costume jewelry can be purchased at reasonable prices. Also, take note of the fiber content of the clothing you plan to purchase. The fiber content is important to the garment's sustainability and quality.

Editing your wardrobe is an ongoing process. This is the mantra I live by: with every item I add, I must discard one. This goes for shoes and bags as well. Be ever ready to continue to declutter, and do have a maintenance plan.

Key Investment Pieces

While sipping my coffee in my local café, I came across an article that listed some key investment pieces worth purchasing. Every piece was by a well-known designer: Chanel, Gucci, Yves Saint Laurent, Max Mara, Christian Louboutin, Cartier, and others. I had to smile when I added up the total cost. The designer investment pieces totaled $28,000. Oh my! This would be a house deposit in some cities! Honestly, a beautiful closet does not need to be filled with designer labels that break the bank. A versatile collection of clothing can be built with affordable pieces! Some advice I was given some time ago was to buy little but buy well! This can be done by following the example of French women and putting more money into key investment pieces.

Here is a list of key wardrobe pieces that are an investment and that are worth paying a higher price for. Use it as a guide. Your list may vary from this depending on your lifestyle.

- The iconic little black dress (LBD) is worth owning, because it can be worn on multiple occasions. Designer Karl Lagerfeld is credited for saying, "One is never over-dressed or underdressed with a Little Black Dress."[11] One type of LBD is a sheath dress. It transcends differences in women's body

11. Lagerfeld, "One Is Never . . ."

How to Build a Wardrobe the French Way

shapes and is always slimming. Another LBD may be an off-the-shoulder style or one in fancy lace.

- Floral dress—could be a good addition to add an alternative look.
- Blouse/button-down shirt—in white if the color suits you.
- Top—one that takes you from day to night.
- Perfectly fitted T-shirt[s]—once you find a brand that has a great fit, buy an assortment of colors.
- Soft cashmere/wool sweater—a great garment for multiple seasons.
- Cardigan—in a neutral color.
- Tailored jacket/blazer—in leather and/or fabric (plain or textured) in a neutral color. A floral, patterned, or checked blazer is not an ideal basic because it will not combine with other coordinates.
- A trench coat—you will always look stylish on dry or rainy days. It will also keep you warm on cooler days when worn with a sweater and boots.
- Wool/cashmere coat—a fundamental basic for chilly days.
- Pencil or A-line skirt—always looks businesslike.
- Well-cut, tailored trousers—can be worn for work or for a night out. It can be a separate piece or to match with a jacket.
- Dark denim jeans—constructed from high-quality fabric with an emphasis on great fit. This is another great basic. Ripped, distressed, torn jeans are not a timeless style. They are a fad/trend that will fade.
- A great handbag and shoes, sunglasses, a belt, and simple, elegant jewelry pieces are excellent basic items. Parisian women walk everywhere, so quality shoes that do not fall apart are a priority.
- Scarf—a French woman's favorite accessory. Scarves in all variety of colors, patterns, and textures made from cotton,

Appendix 2

silk, cashmere, and wool or a blend of fibers are great mixers and will add pizzazz to any outfit. Then, if you wear the same outfit today that you wore yesterday, no one will notice when you accessorize with a different scarf to create a fresh look.

One piece of advice I read suggested that we only need thirty-seven items in our closet. So I counted mine. Yikes! I had seventy items. And on that day, I had put aside three items as a donation to charity. I certainly do need to follow my own advice.

Lastly, some final wise words from New York author Elizabeth L. Cline: "When every garment has a purpose and every color and cut goes with something else, your wardrobe can carry you through life and style, no matter the occasion."[12]

---

12. Cline, *Conscious Closet*, 94.

Appendix 3
Sustainable Fashion

> There is no beauty in the finest cloth
> if it makes hunger and unhappiness.
>
> MAHATMA GANDHI[1]
>
> As consumers, we have so much power to change the world
> by just being careful in what we buy.
>
> EMMA WATSON[2]

W E all wear clothes. It is a creative form of art, expression, and imagination which can glorify God. At an economic level, people can flourish when they are involved in the manufacturing of clothing because it provides jobs. I am an example of someone who flourishes working in the fashion industry. Yet, this is not everyone's story.

There are many concerns connected with manufacturing, such as environmental issues due to how textiles are manufactured, how textile factories weave fabric, and the making of clothing. Sustainable and ethically produced clothing is something you

---

1. Gandhi, "There Is No Beauty . . ."
2. Emma Watson, qtd. in Gale, *Sustainable(ish) Guide*, 11.

Appendix 3

may know little about yet are interested to learn more about. This topic could be the subject of another book itself. Over the past few years, we have been educated to keep plastic bags out of the environment. Solving the plastic- and paper-bag problem required thoughtful and effective solutions. We are also aware of the massive problems caused by climate change and the need for global, workable solutions. As we consider the topic of ethical and sustainable fashion, it may help many of us who love clothes to have more awareness as consumers so that we make wiser choices in our purchasing.

As creatures, we are to practice caring for the earth and to be agents of good stewardship. We know this because Gen 1:26 tells us how God gave humankind dominion over the earth he created. Part of our responsibility as Christian consumers of fashion, therefore, is to consider how to do sustainable fashion. Questions related to environmental concerns, the manufacturing of clothing, and the issue of clothing being dumped into landfills should concern us, because these things mess up God's creation. Psalm 24:1 clearly tells us, "The earth is the Lord's, and everything in it, and the world, and all who live in it." This verse ought to awaken our awareness as followers of Christ, because God expects us as creatures to care for the land we walk on and not exploit it.

Do you realize that "the clothing industry is the second largest polluter in the world . . . second to oil" according to fashion designer and entrepreneur Eileen Fisher?[3] She said this when receiving an award for her commitment to environmental causes. According to an EcoWatch article, "When we think of pollution, we envision coal power plants, strip-mined mountaintops and raw sewerage piped into our waterways. We do not often think of the shirts on our backs. But the overall impact the apparel industry has on our planet is quite grim."[4] The production of fashion is certainly a complicated business. There are so many people involved, including farmers, weavers/workers at knitting mills, textile dyers, designers, seamstresses, mailmen, advertisers, and retailers. Given

---

3. Eileen Fisher, qtd. in Sweeny, "Fast Fashion," para. 1.
4. Sweeny, "Fast Fashion," para. 4.

this, it can be hard to know if a certain fashion label is ethical or not in their manufacturing practices. Unfortunately, sustainability in fashion is difficult to achieve for many reasons. For one, the manufacturing of clothing can have a harmful effect on people and animals and influence environmental degradation. Additionally, fiber production involves fertilizers, chemicals, pesticides, and toxic dyes which prevent the clothing we dispose of from being biodegradable—i.e., capable of being decomposed when dumped into landfills.[5] Another reason sustainability is difficult to achieve is because of fashion being churned out at a hectic pace. The "fast-fashion" trend mentioned in chapter 5 is particularly concerning because of the demand for cheap, quickly produced clothing mostly made from synthetic material, which is not biodegradable.

In an article about the ethical dilemma of fashion, Siobhan Hegarty notes that according to Joshua Badge, a lecturer at Deakin University, Australia, "fashion as a form of excellence can promote . . . 'human flourishing.'"[6] However, Badge says that "there's almost no way, at the moment, to certify that the clothes we buy and wear every day weren't made using child labour, because no-one is monitoring that."[7] This is because most fashion manufacturing is remote from the consumer, and it does not directly impact us. Therefore, we are unaware of how our garments are manufactured. He continues, "I tell my students when we discuss this in class, 'There's a reason that a shirt only cost, you know, $5, and it's because somewhere along the line, someone is losing out.'"[8] We do not really know if those in the manufacturing chain are ethical or not in their practices and if they pay a garment worker in a country such as Bangladesh or Pakistan a decent wage. There is good reason to think that the fashion industry may have some nonethical practices and may exploit their workers in producing inexpensive, cheap, fast fashion.

5. Sweeny, "Fast Fashion," para. 4.
6. Hegarty, "Fashion Labels," para. 6. Hegarty's words.
7. Joshua Badge, qtd. in Hegarty, "Fashion Labels," para. 15.
8. Joshua Badge, qtd. in Hegarty, "Fashion Labels," para. 17.

Appendix 3

One popular garment most of us love to wear are denim jeans, because they are made from a sturdy, durable textile. Are you aware that denim is "resource-heavy" in its production?[9] In her article, Emily Farra notes that "denim is made from cotton—lots of it—and cotton is often grown with harmful fertilizers and pesticides and requires vast amounts of water to produce. A single pair of jeans might need upwards of 1,800 gallons."[10] Cotton is one of the most widespread fabrics used around the world. You may be led to think that the manufacturing process of cotton does not pollute the environment, but that is not so. This should lead us to rethink how many pairs of jeans we need. There are jean brands which do follow ethical practices, pay fair wages, and provide positive working conditions. One such brand advertises this: "Every pair of denim is created in our cutting-edge facility that adheres to the highest ecological and ethical standards."[11] It's great to know of a brand of jeans that produces denim responsibly. One way they practice responsibility and sustainability is by water reduction and recycling of the water used in production.[12]

Another popular garment many of us wear regularly is a T-shirt. Again, in manufacturing, it can take 2,700 liters (713 gallons) to produce the cotton needed to make a single T-shirt.[13] One brand that has impressed me is a company that has respect for the planet and its people and is producing sustainable clothing from farm to factory to closet. A T-shirt from this brand is durable and does not pill or look shabby or shapeless after a few washes. It will last for years and years and consequently will help minimize landfills. Companies such as these produce good-quality garments. Cheap T-shirts hole easily, stretch out of shape, stain, fade, and may even rip and regularly pill. Then the T-shirt ends up in the trash. Does this sound familiar? Buy high-quality T-shirts and jeans. Low-quality garments are only "sew-sew" (pun intended!).

9. Farra, "10 Sustainable Denim Brands," para. 1.
10. Farra, "10 Sustainable Denim Brands," para. 1.
11. "Our Factory," para. 1.
12. "Our Factory," para. 12.
13. "Handle with Care."

Sustainable Fashion

Another concern is that hundreds, even millions, of store items are returned each year because of bad fit, damages, or customer dissatisfaction. For example, if a consumer returns a jacket with a broken zipper, they receive a replacement jacket. The manufacturer does not fix the broken zipper. Instead, faulty garments pile up and remain in the warehouse. Eventually, they go into landfills. The company The Renewal Workshop endeavors to address this problem and to end waste in outdoor apparel. Their aim is to have zero landfill. To achieve this, they recycle garments by sorting, cleaning, and repairing items, such as a jacket zippers or trim, transforming waste into something of value. The products are then sold to retail and brand partners as recycled, renewed apparel. The high-end-fashion retailer Eileen Fisher is another company that has a thoughtful and ethical approach to the boxes of returned garments from their stores, which amount to around two thousand pieces a week. After the garments are returned, they are sorted by clothing kind, color, and fabric type. Since Eileen Fisher has a well-thought-through philosophy of using ethically sourced materials that are free of harmful dyes, their garments can easily be recycled to elongate the life of a returned item. The garments are radically changed by cleaning, made into something new entirely, or resold with a defect which can be remedied.[14]

Most materials will eventually biodegrade; however, the time it takes will vary depending on the environment, soil, and temperature and whether chemicals and harmful dyes have been used.[15] We do know that natural fibers such as cotton and wool are quicker to break down than nonbiodegradable, synthetic textiles such as polyester, nylon, and spandex. Even clothing made from a natural/synthetic blend is not easily biodegradable. It is alarming to find out that it takes up to two hundred years for some nonbiodegradable fabric to disappear from the environment. It's interesting to note that an apple core takes two months to biodegrade and one to five months for organic cotton material to break down

---

14. Read, "In the Future," paras. 7, 10.
15. Arnett, "How Quickly," paras. 1, 6.

in soil.[16] These facts do warn us as consumers to be thoughtful about the type of material we choose when we purchase clothing.

For the environmentally aware fashionista, some brands offer clothing made from sustainable fabrics. Two popular ones are organic cotton and organic bamboo. These can be cut and sewed into excellent, high-quality garments, and this quality will last for years. In the production of organic fabrics, harmful pesticides are minimized to decrease environmental damage. The sustainability of bamboo is impressive. It is grown without the use of pesticides or chemical fertilizers. It grows quickly and is harvested in three to five years. In addition, its production reduces environmental damage more than other types of fibers and, in particular, synthetics.[17] It is also appealing because it is comfortable to wear and breathable and has good moisture-wicking properties.[18] When buying organic, check your garment label to see if it's certified. Like organic food, organic, eco-friendly clothing is more costly.

It was encouraging to read in a *Vogue* article written by Emily Farra, senior fashion news writer, a prediction that in following years, a better attempt will be made into making new clothes out of old ones. In Farra's view: "A more sustainable fashion industry depends on using what exists, eliminating the problem of clothing in landfills, and reframing the way we value our garments."[19] One image in the article pictured two models standing in front of a recycling facility wearing upcycled and regenerated clothing. The garments were made from old, discarded garments, recut and remade and turned into something of greater value.[20] Two French designers are involved in this project, as well as British designer Stella McCartney. The article tells us how an old, ripped, stained, and out-of-shape T-shirt ready to be tossed into the garbage can

16. Arnett, "How Quickly," para. 8.
17. "Bamboo," fn19, para. 6.
18. "Bamboo," fn19, para. 6.
19. Farra, "Future of Fashion," para. 13.
20. Farra, "Future of Fashion."

Sustainable Fashion

be repurposed into another, up-to-date T-shirt or even housing insulation.[21]

Evrnu is an innovative textile company committed to eliminating waste, lowering the carbon footprint, and saving water.[22] Recently, through Evrnu, regenerated fibers have been made available commercially. Now the Evrnu group is working to break down polyester fibers and to rebuild them into a new kind of engineered fiber which will be environmentally friendly. After a sourcing trip to China, Stacy Flynn was motivated to help the environment. Emily Farra quotes her:

> "We need to get used to looking at things and understanding that nothing actually goes 'away' [when we throw it out]—there is no 'away,'" explains Stacy Flynn, the CEO of Evrnu. She came to that realization nearly a decade ago on a sourcing trip in China, where she found herself in a factory town so polluted she couldn't see her colleague standing next to her through the smog. "I realized how impactful and damaging our industry is to the environment, and began adding up all the millions of yards of fabric I'd made over the course of my career.... I was contributing to the problem," she says. She launched Evrnu in 2015 and recently unveiled a groundbreaking technology that breaks cotton waste down into a liquid, then remakes it into stronger, higher-performing fibers.[23]

It is also encouraging to read how Pickering International, a textile-import company specializing in eco-friendly and sustainable textiles, speaks to the problem of leftover fabrics that would otherwise go into landfills.

> You've heard it: reduce, recycle, and repurpose. We put it into practice by collecting manufacturing overruns, scraps from cutting, rejected dye lots, and fabrics from different mills and sewing factories. These post production materials are sorted, shredded, then blended with

---

21. Farra, "Future of Fashion," para. 13.
22. Farra, "Future of Fashion," para. 5. See also www.evrnu.com.
23. Farra, "Future of Fashion," para. 5; brackets in the original.

Appendix 3

new natural fibers or with recycled polyester from plastic bottles before finally being re-spun into colorful yarns from knitting and weaving. In doing so, we offer you beautiful fabrics otherwise destined for landfill. For us, it's an exceptionally rewarding experience.[24]

We also read of renowned fashion labels that have endorsed the work of Cradle to Cradle design. Simply, the concept of Cradle to Cradle is to give a stamp of approval for goods that are healthy (nontoxic) and of a high quality. Cradle to Cradle investigates what the clothing material is made from and if the material can be upcycled into something else. They also check if the water supply used in production is drinkable again, if renewable energy has been used, and if workers are paid a fair wage and work in healthy conditions. To do this, Cradle to Cradle uses the collective expertise, wisdom, knowledge, and skill of chemical scientists, biology experts, and product designers to reveal if a product material is sustainable or not. If a certain material does not meet the standard, that company can easily modify their product. Nevertheless, Cradle to Cradle does not claim to solve all sustainability problems that the worldwide fashion industry faces.[25]

The fashion industry needs a more sustainable philosophy of its textiles and a better understanding of how the dumping of disregarded clothing into landfills adversely affects the environment. As consumers, we can help by having a minimalist approach to our clothing (encouraged as a lifestyle in Appendix 2) and by having a sustainability mindset. This way, we will throw away less, which will reduce clothing waste that goes into landfills and harms the environment.

To practice sustainability, other than buying less clothing, we need to choose an ethical way to dispose of unwanted clothing. There are numerous ways to do this. Recycle garments by donating them to an op shop, or thrift store. However, it must be noted that not all clothing donations are used by our community. Some are rendered worthless and go into landfills or into the incinerator.

24. "Recycled Fibers."
25. Rowen, "Cradle to Cradle Design."

Sustainable Fashion

Another way is by getting involved in a clothing-exchange system. Yet another example of practicing sustainability is how my sister's friend does it—by turning discarded clothing into children's toys. Another way is to turn redundant clothing in quality fabric, such as a dress or skirt, into cushion covers. Then think about turning an old, worn/torn cotton T-shirt into cleaning rags, because it has absorbency. One more way to carry out sustainability is to buy secondhand clothes. Upcycling a few garments into something new was an assignment I set for students in a design course. They were to take several old garments and recut and re-stitch them into one beautiful, new, original garment. I got some genuinely exciting, imaginative designs! Wives of soldiers in WWII also knew how to repurpose clothing rather than disposing of them. They understood how to be resourceful instead of wasteful. As a result, a culture of "make do and mend" emerged, as we read in the following excerpt:

> We had to make do and mend—that was the order of the day, and everything we had got in the wardrobe was kept there, we never threw anything away. I can remember when I was expecting my first baby I was wondering how I could get a christening gown for her and I thought of my wedding dress, but I couldn't bear to put the scissors into it. A few weeks later I went and had another look at it and thought as there was a war on I would have to use it. I got it out and cut a great big piece out of it to make the christening gown, which turned out quite well, and when my little girl was four years old she was in a maypole dancing troupe and she needed a white dress, so I went back to the wedding dress and cut a bit more out of it and made her the little white dress. It was like that with other things like summer dresses.[26]

During the time we self-isolated in Chicago while living through the COVID-19 crisis, I asked Graham to collect the mail from our mailbox on the curb one day (far from our front door), as I still had my pj's on at midday. He said to me, "Just think of your

---

26. Barber, "Make Do and Mend," para. 2.

Appendix 3

pj's as 'quarantine leisure wear.'" I did laugh! Will this be the "new look" after the pandemic? I wonder how and if this COVID-19 pandemic has changed how you view clothing and its sustainability. Perhaps we have learned that rejuvenating your clothes saves money and saves the planet. In my work as a designer recently, a customer came along with her mother's wedding dress, which she wanted upcycled into her daughter's communion dress. The result was magnificent, and the granddaughter looked so gorgeous in her lace dress with all the same details of her grandmother's wedding gown incorporated into the design. This exemplifies sustainability!

Sustainability can also mean stitching some simple repairs by using some basic hand-stitching skills or by using a sewing machine. A too-long hem can be shortened, or long pants can be cut into shorts and stitched, or a hole in your jeans can be mended by placing a patch underneath the hole and machine stitching back and forth until the hole is covered. In lockdown, I am spending time repairing and mending clothes—reinforcing a loose button, darning a hole in the elbow of my sweater—with simple hand sewing using a needle and thread. These are jobs I always put off, as I would prefer to create a new garment than repair an old one, because restoring garments is not creative. As I stitched, I recalled how my father darned holes in his socks during WWII. I never imagined that I would be using the same skill in lockdown in 2020 that my father had learned during the war.

Hopefully, many positive things have come from living through the COVID-19 pandemic when it comes to clothing. Maybe you have rediscovered your sewing machine and sewn some face masks in a variation of styles, or even ones to match your clothing. Perhaps one learning moment has been to discover that you can live with less. Perhaps we have learned that rejuvenating your clothes saves money and help saves the planet. Maybe we will all be more mindful and intentional about what criteria we use to purchase clothing.

Molly Farai, a fashion blogger, rightly says:

> At my very core, I believe that every single person and every business has the power to change the world. So, I

Sustainable Fashion

believe in the power of every fashion brand and I believe in the power of every person who wear clothes to positively impact this world through their choices.

In our capitalist society, our power lies in our money. When we pay for something, we're communicating that we like it. So, whenever you buy new undies, you're telling the brand who is selling them to you that, "hey, I like your product, please make more of it!" And so they do; they make more undies.

So, what happens when those undies are made by the millions, from chemically treated synthetic polyester, made by people who aren't being paid a living wage, in a factory that is unsafe to work in, sold for $2 a pair, designed to fall to pieces in a month, making you buy *more and more and more, constantly?*[27]

To follow this wise advice, buy fewer cheap things and then buy well-made clothes in sustainable fabrics. As consumers of fashion, to address the environmental and sustainability question, perhaps we could start by taking responsibility in how we shop. If possible, prior to buying something, research the brand to find out if they have sustainable design practices and whether ethical industry standards were used in production. Only buy clothes you really love, wear them often, and try not to amass a pile of barely used, not-quite-right jeans, skirts, pants, and dresses or anything else.

---

27. Farai, "Fashion Blogger's Complete Guide," paras. 13–15; italics in the original, boldface removed.

Bibliography

Abrams, Allison. "Shutting Down Body Shame." October 10, 2017. https://www.psychologytoday.com/us/blog/nurturing-self-compassion/201710/shutting-down-body-shaming.

Adams, Ansel. "I Believe the World . . ." https://www.azquotes.com/quote/741076.

Allaire, Christian. "Kate Middleton Recycled One of Her Most Stunning Dresses for the Portrait Gala in London." *Vogue*, March 13, 2019. https://www.vogue.com/vogueworld/article/kate-middleton-2019-portrait-gala-alexander-mcqueen-dress.

———. "Taylor Swift Joins TikTok—And Her Dress Instantly Sells Out." *Vogue*, August 24, 2021. https://www.vogue.com/article/taylor-swift-joins-tiktok-reformation-dress.

Aniston, Jennifer. "I Think Our Bodies . . ." https://www.harpersbazaar.com/fashion/designers/a1576/50-famous-fashion-quotes/.

Apfel, Iris. "These Are Things . . ." https://quotefancy.com/quote/1545845/Iris-Apfel-These-are-things-I-love-things-I-ve-worn-I-get-more-compliments-on-accessories.

Arnett, George. "How Quickly Do Fashion Materials Biodegrade?" *VogueBusiness*, November 29, 2019. https://www.voguebusiness.com/sustainability/fashion-biodegradable-material-circularity-cotton?amp.

Augustine. *The Confessions*. Edited by Philip Schaff. Translated by J. G. Pilkington. Nicene and Post-Nicene Fathers 1. Buffalo, NY: Christian Literature Publishing, 1887. Revised and edited for New Advent by Kevin Knight. https://www.newadvent.org/fathers/1101.htm.

———. *On Christian Doctrine*. Translated by D. W. Robertson Jr. New York: Macmillan, 1958.

"Bamboo." https://econation.co.nz/bamboo/.

Barber, Winifred. "Make Do and Mend." December 4, 2005. https://www.bbc.co.uk/history/ww2peopleswar/stories/26/a7527026.shtml.

Barrymore, Drew. "Why I Put My Closet on a Diet (In 6 Simple Steps)." March 8, 2015. https://www.refinery29.com/en-us/drew-barrymore-closet-cleaning-tips.

Bibliography

Bauck, Witney. "Why Fashion Matters: How Christian Fashion Week Could Spur the Church to Engage Clothing beyond Simply Buying It." *Christianity Today*, August 27, 2015. https://www.christianitytoday.com/ct/2015/july-august/why-fashion-matters.html.

Beale, Gregory K. "Eden, the Temple, and the Church's Mission in the New Creation." *Journal of the Evangelical Theological Society* 48 (March 2005) 5–31. https://www.etsjets.org/files/JETS-PDFs/48/48-1/48-1-pp005-031_JETS.pdf.

"The Best Colors for Neutral Skin Tones—How to Find the Perfect Dress." https://savedbythedress.com/blogs/lifestyle/the-best-colors-for-neutral-skin-tones-how-to-find-the-perfect-dress.

Bhatt, Ananya. "60 Lady in Red Quotes and Captions for Your Instagram Pics." May 16, 2021. https://www.therandomvibez.com/lady-in-red-quotes-captions/.

Bloom, Amy. "You Are Imperfect . . ." http://www.goodreads.com/quotes/tag/body-image.

Boice, James Montgomery. "Why Were Gold, Incense, and Myrrh Appropriate Gifts for Jesus?" December 07, 2010. https://www.crossway.org/articles/why-were-gold-incense-and-myrrh-appropriate-gifts-for-jesus/.

Borrelli-Persson, Laird. "Model Ingmari Lamy Has an Advanced Degree in Boho Chic." *Vogue*, September 5, 2018. https://www.vogue.com/article/model-ingmari-lamy-advanced-style-street-style-stockholm-sweden.

Bowen, Sesali, "Proof That Rhianna Is the Actual Queen of Instagram." May 4, 2017. https://www.refinery29.com/en-us/2017/05/153048/rihanna-instagram-badgalriri-posts-social-influence.

Bowles, Hamish. "Miuccia Prada and Raf Simons: What the Partnership Means for Fashion—and for the New Collaborators Themselves." *Vogue*, February 23, 2020. https://www.vogue.com/article/miuccia-prada-and-raf-simons-what-the-partnership-means-for-fashion.

Brown, Brene. "You Are Imperfect . . ." https://www.goodreads.com/quotes/349410-you-are-imperfect-you-are-wired-for-struggle-but-you.

Brown, Nicole. "Why Creative Thinkers and Artistic Outlets in Society Are More Important Than Ever." June 21, 2017. https://www.skyword.com/contentstandard/creativity/creative-thinking-artistic-outlets-society-important-ever/.

Bruce-Lockhart, Anna. "5 Countries with the Strictest Dress Codes." January 7, 2016. https://www.weforum.org/agenda/2016/01/5-countries-with-the-strictest-dress-codes.

"Buy Less, Choose Well, Make It Last." May 22, 2020. https://www.be-quality.com/en/buy-less-choose-well-make-it-last-vivienne-westwood/.

Calasibetta, Charlotte Mankey, and Phyllis G. Tortora. *The Fairchild Dictionary of Fashion*. 3rd ed. New York: Fairchild, 2003.

Calvin, John. *Institutes of the Christian Religion*. Translated by Henry Beveridge. https://www.ccel.org/ccel/calvin/institutes.

Bibliography

Carson, D. A., ed. *NIV Biblical Theology Study Bible: Following God's Redemptive Plan As It Unfolds Throughout Scripture*. Grand Rapids: Zondervan, 2018.

Castelfranchi, Cristiano. "Six Critical Remarks on Science and the Construction of the Knowledge Society." *Journal of Science Communication* 6 (December 2007). https://doi.org/10.22323/2.06040303.

Chanel, Coco. "Adornment, What a Science! . . ." https://quotefancy.com/quote/788755/Coco-Chanel-Adornment-what-a-Science-Beauty-what-a-weapon-Modesty-what-elegance.

―――. "Fashion Is Not . . ." https://www.goodreads.com/quotes/12859-fashion-is-not-something-that-exists-in-dresses-only-fashion.

Chase, Mitchell L. "A True and Greater Boaz: Typology and Jesus in the Book of Ruth." *Southern Baptist Journal of Theology* 21 (Spring 2017) 85–96. https://equip.sbts.edu/publications/journals/journal-of-theology/sbjt-211-spring-2017/true-greater-boaz-typology-jesus-book-ruth/.

Cheng-Tozun, Dorcas. "Enoch Ho." *Christianity Today*, June 23, 2016. https://www.christianitytoday.com/ct/2016/julaug/enoch-ho.html.

Cherylyoung. "Coco Chanel, Here Are Some of Her Most Famous Quote." *Norma Jeans' Closet* (blog), April 6, 2015. https://normajeansclosetdotorg.wordpress.com/2015/04/06/coc-chanel-here-are-some-of-her-most-famous-quote/.

"Christian Fashion Week Releases Its Initial Designer Lineup for 2015 Final Season Showcase." January 14, 2015. http://www.christianfashionweek.com/Blog/Christian-Fashion-Week-Blog/Christian-Fashion-Week-Blog/Christian-Fashion-Week-Releases-Its-Initial-Designer-Lineup-for-2015-Final-Season-Showcase/?link=1&fldKeywords=&fldAuthor=&fldTopic=0.

"Classy Women Sayings and Quotes." http://www.wiseoldsayings.com/classy-women-quotes/.

Cline, Elizabeth L. *The Conscious Closet: The Revolutionary Guide to Looking Good While Doing Good*. New York: Plume, 2019.

Clowney, E. P. *The Message of 1 Peter: The Way of the Cross*. Bible Speaks Today. Downers Grove, IL: InterVarsity, 1988.

Cocozza, Paula. "Skinny Jeans: The Fashion Trend That Refuses to Die." *Guardian*, January 9, 2013. https://www.theguardian.com/fashion/2013/jan/09/skinny-jeans-fashion-trend-refuses-to-die.

Cole, Julie, and Sharon Czachor. *Professional Sewing Techniques for Designers*. 2nd ed. New York: Fairchild, 2014.

"Color & Culture Matters." https://colormatters.com/color-symbolism/color-and-culture-matters.

Cyprian of Carthage. "Treatise 2." Edited by Alexander Roberts. Translated by Robert Ernest Wallis. In *Fathers of the Third Century: Hippolytus, Cyprian, Caius, Novatian, Appendix*, edited by Arthur Cleveland Coxe et al. Ante-Nicene Fathers 5. Buffalo, NY: Christian Literature, 1886. Revised and edited for New Advent by Kevin Knight. http://www.newadvent.org/fathers/050702.htm.

Bibliography

Entwistle, Joanne, "Dress for Success." https://fashion-history.lovetoknow.com/fashion-clothing-industry/dress-success.

Epicurus. "Do Not Spoil . . ." https://www.goodreads.com/quotes/169009-do-not-spoil-what-you-have-by-desiring-what-you.

Erickson, Dan. "Joshua Becker on Christianity and Becoming a Minimalist." *Hip Diggs* (blog), July 30, 2016. http://www.hipdiggs.com/joshua-becker-christianity-minimalism/.

Falsani, Cathleen. "Bono and Guggi: A Friendship Based on Art, Punk Rock and Jesus." Religion News Service, August 6, 2019. https://religionnews.com/2019/08/06/bono-and-guggi-a-friendship-based-on-art-punk-rock-and-jesus/.

"Famous Fashion Quotes." December 31, 2010. https://famousfashionquotes.tumblr.com/.

Farai, Molly. "A Conscious Fashion Blogger's Complete Guide to Ethical and Sustainable Clothing." *Conscious Clothing* (blog), May 21, 2020. https://www.mfarai.com/a-conscious-fashion-bloggers-complete-guide-to-ethical-and-sustainable-clothing/.

Farra, Emily. "The Future of Fashion Is Circular: Why the 2020s Will Be about Making New Clothes Out of Old Ones." *Vogue*, December 19, 2019. https://www.vogue.com/article/sustainability-2020s-circular-fashion-textile-recycling.

———. "Get to Know the 2018 CFDA/Vogue Fashion Fund Finalists." *Vogue*, July 27, 2018. https://www.vogue.com/article/cfda-vogue-fashion-fund-2018-finalists-interviews.

———. "Loungewear Is Suddenly All-Day-Wear—and Lunya Was Ready for It." *Vogue*, May 29, 2020. https://www.vogue.com/article/lunya-loungewear-ashley-merrill-interview.

———. "These Are the 10 Sustainable Denim Brands You Should Know about Now." *Vogue*, April 24, 2020. https://www.yahoo.com/lifestyle/9-sustainable-denim-brands-know-162236660.html.

———. "What's Selling During the Pandemic? The Answers Might Surprise You." *Vogue*, August 25, 2020. https://www.vogue.com/article/the-realreal-resale-report-pandemic-designers-trends.

Feldon, Leah. *Does This Make Me Look Fat? The Definitive Rules for Dressing Thin for Every Height, Size, and Shape.* New York: Villard, 2003.

Field, David H. "Modesty." In *New Dictionary of Christian Ethics & Pastoral Theology*, edited by David J. Atkinson et al., 599. Downers Grove, IL: InterVarsity, 1995.

Flyyn, Caitlin. "Here's How Retouched Photos Impact Our Mental Health." *Insider*, March 30, 2018. https://www.businessinsider.com/how-retouched-photos-impact-our-mental-health-2018-3.

Ford, Leighton. *A Life of Listening: Discerning God's Voice and Discovering Our Own.* Downers Grove, IL: InterVarsity, 2019.

Fortini, Amanda. "She's a Woman." *Elle*, March 25, 2013. https://www.elle.com/fashion/personal-style/a12555/fashion-trends-women-pant-suit/.

Bibliography

"46 Amazing Quotes about Inner Beauty." https://quotabulary.com/amazing-quotes-about-inner-beauty.
Francis of Assisi. "He Who Works . . ." https://www.goodreads.com/quotes/75455-he-who-works-with-his-hands-is-a-laborer-he.
Franklin, Benjamin. "Money Has Never…" https://www.brainyquote.com/quotes/benjamin_franklin_165453.
Freedman, Judi. "IRIS, a Fabulous Film about a 90+ Fashionista." *HuffPost* (blog), May 14, 2016. http://www.huffingtonpost.com/judi-freedman/iris-a-fabulous-film-about-a-90fashionista_b_7275300.html.
"Frequently Asked Questions." https://www.stjohnsvancouver.org/service-faq.
Fürstenburg, Diane von. "It's the Woman . . ." https://www.azquotes.com/quote/875252.
Gaiser, Frederick J. "What Luther *Didn't* Say about Vocation." *Word & World* 25 (Fall 2005) 359–61. https://wordandworld.luthersem.edu/content/pdfs/25-4_Work_and_Witness/25-4_Editorial.pdf.
Gale, Jen. *The Sustainable(ish) Guide to Green Parenting: Guilt-Free Eco-ideas for Raising Your Kids*. London: Green Tree, 2021.
Gandhi, Mahatma. "There Is No Beauty . . ." https://www.azquotes.com/quote/811260.
Goldstone, Penny. "This Royal's Wedding Dress Took 3,900 Hours to Make." *Marie Claire*, April 14, 2020. https://www.marieclaire.co.uk/fashion/this-royals-wedding-dress-took-3900-hours-to-make-694201.
Gordon, Georgie. "The Fashion Mistake Model Victoria Lee Feels She Still Makes." *Sydney Morning Herald*, August 14, 2021. https://www.smh.com.au/lifestyle/fashion/the-fashion-mistake-model-victoria-lee-feels-she-still-makes-20210811-p58hvi.html.
Grant, Hardie. *Pocket Coco Chanel Wisdom: Witty Quotes and Wise Words from a Fashion Icon*. London: Hardie Grant, 2017.
Gustashaw, Megan. "How to Know What Colors Look Best on You." *GQ*, November 29, 2015. https://www.gq.com/story/how-to-know-what-colors-look-good-on-you.
"Handle with Care." *World Wildlife Magazine*, Spring 2014. https://www.worldwildlife.org/magazine/issues/spring-2014/articles/handle-with-care.
Harper's Bazaar Staff. "The 87 Greatest Fashion Quotes of All Time." *Harper's Bazaar*, February 3, 2022. https://www.harpersbazaar.com/fashion/designers/a1576/50-famous-fashion-quotes/.
Hegarty, Siobhan. "Can Fashion Labels Ever Be Ethical, or Are They Pulling the Wool Over Our Eyes?" ABC Everyday, 28 May, 2019. https://www.abc.net.au/life/can-fashion-labels-ever-be-ethical/11146532.
Hill, Rhonda P. "Did You Know? Non-biodegradable Clothes Take 20 to 200 Years to Biodegrade." https://edgexpo.com/2017/09/05/edge-fast-fact-non-biodegradable-clothes-take-20-to-200-years-to-biodegrade/amp/.

Bibliography

Hoby, Dominique. "Rihanna Is Undoubtably a Fashion Icon, Here's Why." *Essence*, October 27, 2020. https://www.essence.com/celebrity/rihanna-undoubtably-fashion-icon-heres-why/.

Housley, Macharva. "My Five Seasons of Sewing." https://www.sewdaily.com/sewing/my-five-seasons-of-sewing/.

"How Coco Chanel Freed Women from the Tyranny of Victorian Corsets." *Lifestyle Asia*, October 14, 2020. https://www.lifestyleasia.com/hk/style/fashion/how-coco-chanel-freed-women-from-the-tyranny-of-victorian-corsets/.

Hughes, Melina, and Virginia Fitzsimons. "Lessons from Aristotle: All Things in Moderation." *Nursing* 46 (April 2016) 50–53. https://doi.org/10.1097/01.NURSE.0000481422.11588.7e.

Hutton, Lauren. "Fashion Is What ..." https://www.azquotes.com/quote/538499.

Instone-Brewer, David. *Moral Questions of the Bible: Timeless Truth in a Changing World*. Scripture in Context. Bellingham, WA: Lexham, 2019.

"Introducing Cristóbal Balenciaga." V&A, n.d. https://www.vam.ac.uk/articles/introducing-cristobal-balenciaga.

"Is There a Dress Code?" https://www.stjohnsvancouver.org/service-faq.

Jones, Amelie. "History of Art and Fashion: With Art and Fashion Collaborating Like Never Before, We Look at Some of History's Most Important Crossovers . . ." *We Heart*, September 20, 2021. https://www.we-heart.com/2021/09/20/history-art-and-fashion/.

Juma, Norbet. "Fashion Quotes Celebrating Design and Your Favorite Designers." May 9, 2022. https://everydaypower.com/fashion-quotes/.

Juneau, Jen. "Kelly Clarkson Jokes about How Having 'Tight Pants' after Holiday Weight Gain Is 'So Worth It.'" December 31, 2018. https://people.com/health/kelly-clarkson-holiday-weight-gain-tight-pants-worth-it/.

Keller, Timothy. "If you have money, power, and status today, it is largely due to the century and place in which you were born, to your talents and capacities and health . . ." Facebook, January 2, 2018. https://www.facebook.com/TimKellerNYC/posts/1726378144068731.

Kosloski, Philip. "How Was Baptism Practiced in the Early Church?" April 26, 2019. https://aleteia.org/2019/04/26/how-was-baptism-practiced-in-the-early-church/.

Kruse, Colin G. *John: An Introduction and Commentary*. Tyndale New Testament Commentaries 4. Downers Grove, IL: InterVarsity, 2017.

Lagerfeld, Karl. "One Is Never ..." https://www.goodreads.com/quotes/324628-one-is-never-over-dressed-or-underdressed-with-a-little-black.

Lane, Thomas J. "Jesus as High Priest: The Significance of the Seamless Robe." July 19, 2019. https://stpaulcenter.com/jesus-as-high-priest-the-significance-of-the-seamless-robe/.

Leitch, Luke. "A Man's Guide to a Woman's Wardrobe." *Economist*, September 9, 2011. https://www.economist.com/prospero/2011/09/09/a-mans-guide-to-a-womans-wardrobe.

Bibliography

"Living Your Faith Through Stewardship: Your Time, Talent and Treasure." www.staindy.org/church/files/2013/04/Week-8-10-Stewardship-of-Treasure.pdf.

Long, April. "The Totality: Rihanna." *Elle*, September 26, 2017. https://www.elle.com/culture/celebrities/a12119568/rihanna-the-totality-cover-story-october-2017/.

Lynnette. "Garages Aren't for Cars Anymore." *DIY Household Tips Guide* (blog). https://household-tips.thefuntimesguide.com/garages_filled_with_stuff/.

Manning, Charles. "14 Important Lessons I've Learned as a Fashion Editor." August 4, 2015. https://www.cosmopolitan.com/style-beauty/fashion/advice/a44235/important-lessons-ive-learned-as-a-fashion-editor/.

Marshall, I. Howard. *1 Peter*. IVP New Testament Commentary Series 17. Downers Grove, IL: InterVarsity, 1991.

Martin, J. J. "Carolina Herrera on Selfie Etiquette and Airport Style." *Wall Street Journal*, November 12, 2015. https://www.wsj.com/articles/carolina-herrera-on-selfie-etiquette-and-airport-style-1447349268.

Mather, Katie. "Influencer Shows Society's 'Ideal Body' Evolution." https://www.intheknow.com/post/fitness-influencer-shows-the-perfect-body-evolution-throughout-the-decades/.

Meagher, David. *Fashion Speak: Interviews with the World's Leading Designers*. North Sydney, NSW: Random House Australia, 2008.

"Megan Fox Measurements." http://gossipmagazines.net/megan-fox-measurements/.

Miller, Darrow. "WANTED: God's Fashion Designers." *Darrow Miller and Friends* (blog), November 12, 2012 http://darrowmillerandfriends.com/2012/11/12/gods-fashion-designer/.

Newcomb, Alyssa. "Katie Holmes' Style for Summer 2020 Is Effortlessly Chic." August 3, 2020. https://www.today.com/style/katie-holmes-style-summer-2020-effortlessly-chic-t188341.

Oleic. "Why Creativity Is Just as Important as Literacy." May 1, 2019. https://medium.com/oleicverse/why-creativity-is-just-as-important-as-literacy-59ba7b36b10.

"Our Factory." https://warpweftworld.com/pages/our-factory.

"Our Story." https://warpweftworld.com/pages/our-story.

Pagoto, Sherry. "How to Stop Hating Your Body: Body Dissatisfaction Is the One-Size-Fits-All Epidemic." September 9, 2014. https://www.psychologytoday.com/intl/blog/shrink/201409/how-stop-hating-your-body.

Park, Alice. "In Pictures: Traditional Dress around the World." August 31, 2021. https://www.roughguides.com/gallery/traditional-dress/.

Phelps, Nicole. "Narciso Rodriguez at 20—The Designer Reminisces with a Capsule Collection That Re-creates His Hits." *Vogue*, February 1, 2018. https://www.vogue.com/article/narciso-rodriguez-barneys-20-years-capsule-collection.

Bibliography

Picard, Rosaland. "An MIT Professor Meets the Author of All Knowledge." *Christianity Today*, March 15, 2019. https://www.christianitytoday.com/ct/2019/april/rosalind-picard-mit-professor-meets-author-knowledge.html.

PsychAlive. "I Hate My Body: Dealing with Poor Body Image." https://www.psychalive.org/i-hate-my-body/.

Puente, Maria. "Here Come the Meghan Markle Royal Wedding Gown Knockoffs." *USA Today*, May 25, 2018. https://www.usatoday.com/story/life/2018/05/25/meghan-markles-royal-wedding-gown-knockoffs-ready-take-off/638720002/.

Queen, Nancy. "How Many Clothes Should a Woman Have in Her Wardrobe?" *Shopping on Champagne* (blog). https://www.shoppingonchampagne.com/blog/how-many-clothes-should-a-woman-have-in-her-wardrobe.

Read, Bridget, "In the Future, We'll All Be Wearing Eileen Fisher." *Vogue*, May 29, 2019. https://www.vogue.com/article/in-the-future-we-will-all-be-wearing-eileen-fisher.

"Recycled Fibers." http://picknatural.com/eco-fibers/recycled-fibers/.

Ro, Christine. "Can Fashion Ever Be Sustainable?" BBC, March 11, 2020. https://www.bbc.com/future/article/20200310-sustainable-fashion-how-to-buy-clothes-good-for-the-climate.

Rosner, Brian S. "Biblical Theology." In *New Dictionary of Biblical Theology*, edited by T. Desmond Alexander and Brian S. Rosner, 3–10. Leicester, UK: InterVarsity, 2000.

Rowen, Brendon. "Evolving Responsible Fashion with Cradle to Cradle Design." February 3, 2016. http://www.c2c-centre.com/news/evolving-responsible-fashion-cradle-cradle-design.

Rowling, J. K. "'Fat' Is Usually . . ." https://www.goodreads.com/quotes/tag/j-k-rowling.

Rubenstein, Hal. "Designer Focus: Victoria Beckham on Her Latest Line and How a Woman Can Find Her Signature Style." *InStyle*, October 24, 2013. https://www.instyle.com/news/designer-focus-victoria-beckham-her-latest-line-and-how-woman-can-find-her-signature-style.

Ryken, Leland, et al. *Dictionary of Biblical Imagery*. Electronic ed. Downers Grove, IL: InterVasity, 2000.

Saint Laurent, Yves. "Over the Years . . ." https://www.brainyquote.com/quotes/yves_saint_laurent_389635#:~:text=Yves%20Saint%20Laurent%20Quotes&text=Over%20the%20years%20I%20have%20learned%20that%20what%20is%20important,woman%20who%20is%20wearing%20it.

Samaha, Barry, and Shelby Ying Hyde. *Harper's Bazaar*, July 7, 2021. https://www.harpersbazaar.com/fashion/designers/g32971271/best-coco-chanel-quotes/.

Sardone, Antonia. "Equality: How the Fashion Industry Is Supporting the LGBTQ+ Community & Women's Rights." June 26, 2022. https://www.universityoffashion.com/blog.

Bibliography

Schaeffer, Edith. *Hidden Art*. Wheaton, IL: Tyndale, 1982.

Schaeffer, Francis A. *Art and the Bible*. Downers Grove, IL: InterVarsity, 2006.

Scott, Jess C. "The Human Body . . ." https://www.goodreads.com/quotes/300524-the-human-body-is-the-best-work-of-art.

———. "When Someone Loves You . . ." https://www.goodreads.com/author/quotes/2980674.

Searls, Danielle Peterson. "Crusader Chic." *Lapham's Quarterly*. https://www.laphamsquarterly.org/fashion/crusader-chic.

Seid, Shayna. "101 Fashion Quotes So Timeless They're Basically Iconic." June 17, 2020. https://stylecaster.com/feature/fashion-quotes-203026/.

Siebert-Hommes, Jopie. "The Symbolic Function of Clothing in the Book of Esther." Revised version of a paper presented at the SBL International Meeting in Rome, July 2001. http://www.lectio.unibe.ch/02_1/siebert.htm.

Simon, Samantha. "12 Things to Know about Our Style Crush, Jenna Coleman." *InStyle*, May 13, 2017. https://www.instyle.com/celebrity/12-things-know-about-our-style-crush-jenna-coleman.

Smith, Kate. "Symbolic Colors of India." http://www.sensationalcolor.com/color-meaning/color-around-the-world/india-country-symbolic-colors-1935#.WPjYSYWcHIU.

Stampler, Laura. "The Bizarre History of Women's Clothing Sizes." *Time*, October 23, 2014. https://time.com/3532014/women-clothing-sizes-history/.

"The Standard." https://www.global-standard.org/the-standard.html.

Stevens, Connie. "Nothing You Wear . . ." https://www.brainyquote.com/quotes/connie_stevens_197013.

"The Struggle Is Real! Infographic Reveals the Average Woman Has 103 Items in Her Closet While Laying Out the Real Reasons She Can Still Never Find Anything to Wear." *Daily Mail*, April 29, 2016. https://www.dailymail.co.uk/femail/article-3564177/The-struggle-real-Infographic-reveals-average-woman-103-ITEMS-closet-laying-REAL-reasons-never-wear.html.

Sweeny, Glynis. "Fast Fashion Is the Second Dirtiest Industry in the World, Next to Big Oil." August 17, 2015. https://www.ecowatch.com/fast-fashion-is-the-second-dirtiest-industry-in-the-world-next-to-big-1882083445.html.

"10 Top Tips for Winning at 'Make Do and Mend.'" https://www.iwm.org.uk/history/10-top-tips-for-winning-at-make-do-and-mend.

Tertullian. "On the Apparel of Women." Translated by S. Thelwall. In *Fathers of the Third Century: Tertullian, Part Fourth, Minucius Felix, Commodian, Origen, Parts First and Second*, edited by Alexander Roberts et al. Ante-Nicene Fathers 4. Buffalo, NY: Christian Literature, 1885. Revised and edited for New Advent by Kevin Knight. http://www.newadvent.org/fathers/0402.htm.

Towner, Philip H. *1–2 Timothy & Titus*. Downers Grove, IL: InterVarsity, 1994.

Bibliography

Valenti, Lauren. "How Staring at Our Faces on Zoom Is Impacting Our Self-Image." *Vogue*, August 3, 2020. https://www.vogue.com/article/body-dysmorphia-zoom-face.

Versace, Gianni. "That Is the Key . . ." https://www.goodreads.com/quotes/1209555-that-is-the-key-of-this-collection-being-yourself-don-t.

"What Is Trinity Knox Classical Academy?" https://trinityknoxclassical.com/about-tkca.

Whelchel, Hugh. "Four Principles of Biblical Stewardship." November 26, 2012. https://tifwe.org/four-principles-of-biblical-stewardship/.

Whitney, Christine. "What Your Bag & Shoes Say About You." *Harper's Bazaar*, September 4, 2014. http://www.harpersbazaar.com/fashion/trends/a3393/what-your-accessories-say-about-you-0914/.

Williamson, Paul R. "Exodus." In *NIV Zondervan Study Bible: Built on the Truth of Scripture and Centered on the Gospel Message*, edited by D. A. Carson. Grand Rapids: Zondervan, 2015.

Wiseman, Eva. "Amazing Grace Coddington: Inside the World of US Vogue's Creative Director." *Guardian*, November 25, 2012. http://www.guardian.co.uk/fashion/2012/nov/25/grace-coddington-memoirs-us-vogue-interview.

"The Women Designers Who Changed the Way We Dress." *Vogue*, August 14, 2019. https://www.vogue.com/article/women-designers-who-changed-the-way-we-dress.

Wright, Tom. *Advent for Everyone: A Journey through Matthew*. London: Society for Promoting Christian Knowledge, 2016.

Yeoman, Greta. "24/7 Faith." *Come Alive*, July 3, 2015. https://alivenz.wordpress.com/2015/07/03/focus-feature-247-faith/.

Yotka, Steff. "The Decade in Fashion—According to the People Who Made It." *Vogue*, December 16, 2019. https://www.vogue.com/slideshow/the-2010s-in-fashion-scrapbook/amp.

Zee, Joe, and Maggie Bullock Edt. *The ELLEments of Personal Style*. New York: Gotham, 2010.

Zimmerman, Eilene. "Roaming the World, Detecting Fashion." *New York Times*, May 11, 2008. https://www.nytimes.com/2008/05/11/jobs/11starts.html.

www.ingramcontent.com/pod-product-compliance
Lightning Source LLC
Chambersburg PA
CBHW050822160426
43192CB00010B/1861